D1456879

❀

Florida Gardening by the Sea

Florida Gardening
by the Sea

MARY JANE McSWAIN

UNIVERSITY PRESS OF FLORIDA

Gainesville Tallahassee Tampa Boca Raton Pensacola Orlando Miami Jacksonville

02 01 00 99 98 97 6 5 4 3 2 1

Library of Congress Cataloging-in-Publication Data
McSwain, Mary Jane
Florida gardening by the sea / Mary Jane McSwain
p. cm.
Includes bibliographical references and index.
ISBN 0-8130-1529-4 (alk. paper)
1. Seaside gardening—Florida. I. Title.
SB543.2.F6M37 1997
635'.09759'09146—dc21 97-19009

The University Press of Florida is the scholarly publishing agency
for the State University System of Florida, comprised of Florida
A & M University, Florida Atlantic University, Florida International
University, Florida State University, University of Central Florida,
University of Florida, University of North Florida, University of
South Florida, and University of West Florida.

University Press of Florida
15 Northwest 15th Street
Gainesville, FL 32611

This book was written especially for Florida gardeners, who sometimes need a little help.

I dedicate it to the memory of my mother, an ardent gardener; my husband, George H. McSwain, M.D., who encouraged me; and Herbert M. Davidson, who talked me into doing something I didn't know I could do—write for a newspaper.

I also dedicate it to Thaddeus "Ted" Cyzycki, foremost local gardening authority, whose generous assistance and expertise have been invaluable; and to Ted's late wife, Dolores, who suggested this book and who offered Ted's help "so that his wealth of knowledge on gardening in the Halifax area would not die when he does."

Contents

Foreword

This book is indispensable for new gardeners and for those new to the coastal gardening environment. For experienced southern gardeners, it is another valuable reference work.

Soon after my move to Florida I met Mary Jane McSwain because of our mutual interest in gardening communication. Her telephone soon became my lifeline when I found my midwest experience in gardening woefully inadequate to cope with Florida's special conditions. Mary Jane's long experience and her years spent answering gardening questions have given her insight into the special problems faced by Florida gardeners. Through her writings and lectures, she has earned the title "Garden Lady of Volusia County."

The organization of the book makes it an invaluable tool for gardeners who need answers to specific problems. Readers can rely on her answers because they come from the author's experience and from her constant association with experts in specialized fields. Her writing style is easy to follow and enjoyable.

I welcome the appearance of this book. With it, Florida transplants like me are certain to find their gardening efforts more productive and pleasurable.

W. J. JUNG
Executive Director, Garden Writers
Association of America, 1984–1991

Preface

Through the ages gardening has been conducive to good mental and physical health. In the past few years medical and rehabilitative concepts have pointed up the need to find ways to motivate patients to help themselves toward health. Initially, horticultural pursuits were stimulated by need. But they have been used more and more in rehabilitation and healing because they are varied and available to all.

Gardening can improve the quality of anyone's life in many ways. Gardeners watch the development of a plant from a tiny seed or the emergence of amazing leaves and blossoms from an ugly bulb. The sex life of plants fascinates us. The mysteries of plants excite our minds. But mastering the subject is not the chief reason why we garden. Those who spend time with growing things experience peace and awe inspired by the well-ordered ways of nature.

Although we may never know the answer to questions such as why leaves have so many shapes or how plants can measure the length of a day, we know that working with plants can help release tensions, melt anxieties, still doubts, diminish troubles, develop responsibilities, and give us a chance to be creative.

Furthermore, when we are lonely, anxious, or bored, we can find relief in gardening. A garden may seem like a place of isolation. Yet nothing you can do offers such rich opportunities for comradeship, friendship, and fellowship. In gardening we find opportunities for families, friends, and neighbors to share and grow together. No one is excluded. All—the elderly and children, the emotionally disturbed and the retarded, heart patients, the blind and deaf, and those with other physical handicaps—can find encouraging activities from some form of gardening.

Our gardens not only provide food that is more healthful, fresher, and tastier than what we buy in a supermarket, but growing our own food also saves money while enriching and beautifying the land. Moreover, gardening reflects better things to come. Just as life is enriched by an appreciation of music, so it is enhanced by the knowledge and enjoyment of the garden. Gardeners develop a sense of reverence about its intricate complexity and ultimate simplicity.

I hope that you will find the same kind of mental, physical, and aesthetic satisfaction that I have enjoyed through gardening. Gardeners live close to nature and find every rising sun exciting. If you follow the simple instructions in this book, I promise that you can gain health, happiness, and success as a southeastern seacoast gardener.

So get out into the garden, even if you don't do anything more than hug a hibiscus!

❀

I wish to express my gratitude to those who have assisted me in making this book possible, particularly Thaddeus "Ted" Cyzycki for gardening knowledge; Dr. Robert J. Black of the University of Florida Cooperative Extension Service for advice; Becky and Mike Cyzycki for research; the *Daytona Beach News-Journal* for its cooperation; Paul Ecke Ranch of Encinitas, California, for permission to use *Ten Steps for Success with House-plant Poinsettias;* Kistler London for editing and design; Ruth Matheny for editing; John McSwain for computer instruction; Kitty Tarelis for artwork; Tom Underwood of Disney World Horticulture Services for advice and editing; and Alice Strickland, Volusia County historian, for her unwavering confidence in my ability to produce this book.

Introduction

I wrote this book to supply basic information for succeeding at sea-coast gardening with the greatest ease and in the shortest possible time. The fundamentals in this book were developed in the greater Halifax area on the eastern coast of Florida, where differences between growing plants close to the sea and growing them inland present exciting challenges.

Gardening along any seacoast has always created special problems. Plants are subject to salt spray, salt in groundwater, inadequate and erratic rainfall, wind, and infertile soils. Seacoast gardening must adapt to all of these conditions plus drastic weather changes that may go from hot to cold, dry to wet, and back again. This produces a hostile environment for most growing things. (See the section on soil in chapter 1 for an explanation of pH and infertility.)

In the infertile coastal soils, we are faced with all the problems that come with planting in highly alkaline, porous earth that has little organic content. Soils in the first-line zone, within five hundred feet of the beach, are practically devoid of organic material because at one time they formed the bottom of the ocean.

Furthermore, it is fair to say that ocean water is not conducive to growing most plants. Florida is surrounded on three sides by salt water. But fresh water is the critical natural resource needed in abundance by industry and recreation, as well as by agriculture. Fortunately, low-lying Florida is dotted with numerous freshwater lakes and rivers. However, many are connected to the ocean, meaning that geography and topography pose special problems in control and management of available water. The encroaching danger is saltwater intrusion. Formerly the water table containing salt water was several hundred feet below the surface. Now salt water is found at much higher levels. When extensive fresh water is pumped off, salt water rises to take its place. This intrusion has been compounded by scarcity of rain and ever-increasing numbers of deep wells.

But don't let these facts frighten you away from gardening. Dooryard gardeners can overcome the rigors of the seacoast environment. In fact, with proper management, it's possible to garden year round in Florida—and up the eastern seaboard as far as North Carolina.

A successful gardener uses a combination of supplementary organic materials, acid fertilizers, cover crops, crop rotation, and proper irrigation to keep soils in a condition adequate for growing plants.

Seacoast gardens fall into a wide range of categories, from a container on a condominium balcony to extensive acreage. Regardless of size, there is something for everyone. Dooryard landscaping has taken on a new look as the economy has placed constraints on money and space. More edible fruits and vegetables are incorporated into overall plans. Food and flowers have become friends, joining forces to complement each other. A salad or herb garden serves as a border planting or enhances a window box. Vegetables are tucked around annuals and shrubbery. Grape arbors function as shady spots for warm days. Fruit trees double as ornamentals.

Native plant life in the southeastern part of the United States is remarkable. It's possible to landscape your grounds entirely by using plants found in the wild. Of course, these must not be acquired without permission of the owner on whose land they grow, nor can they be taken from a park or an area protected by law. However, more than three thousand species of "wild plants," not including the cultivated forms, are grown for horticultural purposes. There are specific rules governing the 255 endangered species listed for Florida.

Outdoor living is high on the list of reasons why many people establish permanent residences along the southeastern seacoast. Newcomers find most days bright and sunny and the people warm and friendly. Our homes are just as inviting and pleasant outdoors as they are inside because the majority of homeowners do some form of gardening. A garden is a place for exercise and relaxation; a place to watch birds, butterflies, and squirrels; and a place to grow fruit and vegetables to supplement and enrich table fare. Gardeners are usually happy, contented, pleasant people who add to the beauty and productiveness of society in general. They have learned that gardening is like an investment with a high rate of return.

CHAPTER I

❀

Basics You Need to Know

A Gardener's Vocabulary

Modern classifications in biology are based on the work of a Swedish botanist, Carl von Linne, also known as Carolus Linnaeus (1707–78). He is considered the father of modern botany and a pioneer in plant study. Linnaeus discovered order and meaning in nature by studying plants, and he gave each a double name using the genus and species. His reason for naming plants was a practical one—to provide an accurate means for putting a verbal handle on a plant.

Linnaeus used Latin in classifications because it was the language used in earlier systems and because the meaning of Latin names does not change. Therefore, the name in Latin is the same in all parts of the world.

The basic category, known as *genus,* is composed of related plants that resemble one another and are able to breed among themselves but are not able to breed with members of another genus. The first name of a plant reveals its genus. The second name shows the *species* and indicates a group of closely related varieties within a genus, making a family of plants. The first name, the genus, should be capitalized and the second name, the species, lowercased. Here is an example: *Acer rubrum,* the red maple.

Linnaeus gave each species a name that was descriptive of the plant or told the locality in which it grew. For example, *Magnolia grandiflora* was named for Pierre Magnol, an early French botanist, and *grandiflora* means "large-flowered." *Gardenia jasminoides* was named for Alexander Garden, a physician in Charleston, and *jasminoides* means "jasmine-like," telling us that the plant has a sweet odor.

Most genuses have a number of species. For instance, the *Magnolia* genus includes such flowers as *M. grandiflora* (flowers that are large), *M. liliflora* (flowers like a lily), and *M. stellata* (flowers like a star).

Once you break down the botanical names and see how they are put together, they begin to make sense.

The origins of the names of many species are obvious, including *pro-stratum* (prostrate), *compacta* (compact), *spinosa* (spines), *fragrans* (fragrant), *pendula* (hanging down), and *serrata* (notched edges).

Because this book was written for dooryard gardeners and not for professionals, the use of botanical names is limited. They can be identified by italics and are used only when I am not aware of a common name or for some other specific reason. Now I hope that you will feel more at ease when confronted with the Latin name of a plant.

Garden Vocabulary

The following glossary consists of simple terms that will help you better understand the information in this book. Knowing the meaning of gardening terms won't make you a seasoned gardener, but it will help you think like one and understand and appreciate nature more.

Annuals, biennials, and perennials. Plants are classified as annuals, biennials, or perennials according to their life cycles. Some may fall into more than one of these categories depending on the weather, climate, soil, and care. Many have been hybridized to such an extent that it is difficult to determine just which group they belong in.

Annuals grow from seeds and bloom in a single season but die after they flower and set seeds. Examples are ageratum, bachelor's button, calendula, celosia, cosmos, forget-me-not, marigold, nasturtium, petunia, pansy, sweet alyssum, snapdragon, statice, stock, sweet pea, salvia, strawflower, and sunflower.

Annuals are used to provide color in beds, borders, window boxes, and hanging baskets. Most of our cut flowers are annuals. Cutting the flowers from annual plants stimulates the production of more buds. This is because the primary function of flowers is to produce seeds to keep the species going. When plants "go to seed," they stop blooming and will die.

Biennials grow from seeds and usually live and bloom through two seasons before dying. They may grow for two years before flowering and then die. They usually don't bloom more than once; otherwise, they are considered short-lived perennials. Examples are dianthus, hollyhock, larkspur, poppy, and stock. Sweet alyssum, salvia, and marigolds can live and flower for two years under ideal conditions but are classified as annuals.

Perennials can live and bloom for years under suitable conditions. Many require annual pruning, some have to be dug and divided in two to five years, some are evergreens, and some are deciduous (they lose their leaves during their dormant season). With planned selections of species that bloom at various seasons, your garden can be colorful throughout the year with perennials such as black-eyed Susan, day lily, carnation, chrysanthemum, dahlia, delphinium, ginger, gazania daisy, Shasta daisy, and gaillardia.

Balled and burlapped. This means leaving a ball of soil around the roots of a plant to minimize root damage during moving and transplanting. The ball is usually encased in burlap or similar material.

Bare root. This describes the way in which many varieties of deciduous plants are sold in winter or early spring. All of the soil is carefully removed from the roots of dormant plants. The roots are cleaned, trimmed, and kept moist until they can be replanted.

Companion planting. This means growing different plants in the same area at the same time for the benefit of each other. For example, it is thought that garlic, onions, and marigolds, placed near other plants, will deter pests. Companion planting also includes interplanting fast-maturing vegetables among slow-growing vegetables, such as radishes with lettuce, leaf lettuce with tomatoes and carrots, carrots with peas, corn with beans, and basil with tomatoes.

Complete fertilizers. These fertilizers contain all three primary plant nutrients absorbed by roots: nitrogen, phosphorus, and potassium—the three numbers on the fertilizer bags.

Container-grown plants. These are plants grown in some type of container. Advantages of this method are that plants get a better start in life, are easier to transport and transplant, and receive less shock when transplanted.

Cultivar. This is a plant produced by human intervention such as cross-pollination (hibiscus). Sometimes cultivars may be created from a mutant specimen (rose) with unusual characteristics by dividing plants or rooting cuttings.

Damping off. This term describes a disease caused by a fungus in the soil that makes new seedlings wilt and die. Soil-borne fungi are encouraged by excessive moisture, high humidity, warm temperatures, and insufficient sunshine. Petunias are especially vulnerable. Disinfecting the soil, careful watering practices, good drainage, and spraying with a fungicide will control the problem.

Deciduous. These trees and shrubs drop their leaves and remain leafless during their dormant period. Leaf drop is determined by season—cool and/or dry.

Dormancy. This term refers to a cycle period that occurs as winter nears, days grow shorter, and temperatures drop, allowing a plant to slow down its growth process and rest. The period ends in spring, when plants are exposed to higher temperatures for an extended number of hours.

Drip line. This term is associated with watering and fertilizing trees and shrubs and indicates a line drawn around a tree directly under the outermost ends of branches, where rainwater drips off.

Espalier. This is a pruning technique used to train plants to grow flat against a surface, such as a wall or a trellis, as a space saver or for aesthetic reasons.

Exotic. This term indicates plants introduced to a region in which they are not native. The word does *not* mean unusually beautiful, different, or rare.

Flat. A flat is a shallow plastic, metal, or wooden box used to make a seed bed in which to sprout seeds. When the seeds grow into plantlets, they can then be set out in the garden. A flat is usually three to four inches deep, fourteen inches wide, and twenty-four inches long.

More efficient flats come with a clear plastic lid for even moisture control and rapid germination.

Foliar feeding. This is a process by which nutrients are applied to the leaves of plants using spray applications of soluble fertilizers that have a low burn potential. Sometimes when plants don't absorb necessary elements from the soil through their roots, spraying the foliage with liquid fertilizer can give them a boost and start them on a normal course.

Hardening off. This is the process of slowing plant growth in the fall by withholding water, lowering the temperature, and using a low-nitrogen fertilizer. The method is also used to increase chances for survival when transplanting or when moving plants from a protected environment to a more rigorous outdoor life.

Hardy plants. These are strong, sturdy, healthy plants that have the ability to resist frost, salt, wind, drought, and general neglect. Examples are agave, asparagus fern, beach daisy, bush daisy, cactus, coontie, dianthus, elaeagnus, gaillardia, India hawthorn, juniper, pampas grass, pitto-sporum, photinia, podocarpus, portulaca, purslane, stock, vinca, and yucca.

Heading and pinching back. These pruning methods involve the wise removal of parts of plants to obtain a more desirable plant. *Heading* is pruning back a branch to a bud or a side branch in order to make it bushier. *Pinching* is nipping off just the tips of branches with the thumb and forefinger to increase side growth and make plants bushier.

Herbicide. This term refers to any chemical used to destroy undesirable plants, especially weeds. Some herbicides kill on contact with stems and leaves (postemergents), while others have to be absorbed by the roots of the plant (preemergents). Preemergents are applied when preparing the soil for planting. Some herbicides are selective; others will kill everything they come into contact with. These substances must be used with caution.

Herbaceous plants. These plants have soft, usually green, nonwoody stems.

Hybrid. This term refers to a plant that results from crossing two unlike varieties or species possessing different individual characteristics with the intention of producing specific desirable traits from each. Hybrids are often exceptionally vigorous and healthy but do not breed true—that is, you can't grow hybrids from hybrid-produced seed. Many hybrids are infertile.

Inorganic, organic, and organic gardening. These are terms used to classify specific chemical compounds and a style of gardening.

The word *inorganic* is generally taken to mean chemical compounds or substances, intended for use as soil amendments, composed of matter that is not, and never was, living (animal or vegetable). They are usually man-made rather than from natural growth.

Organic is a term that describes any material of plant or animal origin that contains no man-made chemicals.

Organic gardening refers to a method of growing and maintaining plants without the use of inorganic materials (manufactured chemical pesticides and fertilizers).

Mulch. This is any material applied to the soil surface to conserve soil moisture, maintain an even soil temperature, and aid in weed control. Mulch may be partly decomposed pine needles, compost, straw, leaves, grass clippings, sawdust, paper, or a mixture of several of these materials.

Photosynthesis. This is the process occurring in the leaves of plants in which simple minerals and gases produce carbohydrates. It is accomplished with the help of chlorophyll in the presence of sunlight.

Pesticides/insecticides. These preparations are used for killing insects. They may be of botanical or synthetic origin and should be used with caution.

Root-bound (pot-bound). This occurs when a plant remains too long in a container and its roots become choked. Some plants seem to bloom better when slightly pot-bound, but this condition can inhibit growth and development. When a plant has outgrown its container, remove it from the pot. If the roots seem matted, are circling the pot, or are growing out of the bottom, loosen and lightly prune them to stimulate new development.

Salinity. The amount of salt in groundwater is an ever-growing concern. Any reading above seven hundred parts per million is undesirable for most plants. Some plants can tolerate more salt than others.

Some can tolerate a certain percentage of salt on their roots but not on their foliage.

Succulent plants. These plants have fleshy, juicy tissues. Succulents are usually tolerant of drought because their leaves and stems store water. However, this water storage allows them to freeze easily.

Sp., spp. These are the abbreviations for "species"; *sp.* indicates singular, and *spp.* indicates plural. The same full spelling (species) is used for both. When it is used after the name of a plant, *spp.* indicates there is more than one species of that individual plant from which to choose.

Stock. This refers to a plant used for rootstock. It is a rooted stem on which another plant is grafted.

Sweet/sour. These terms are commonly used when referring to the degree of acidity and alkalinity in the soil. This is determined by the pH reading, which is explained in the section on soil.

Tropical areas. These are areas in which tender plants can survive because temperatures rarely fall below freezing. *Subtropical* are those areas that border on tropical areas and are sometimes subjected to freezing temperatures.

Xeriscape. This is a name used to describe a landscaping technique. The name is derived from the Greek word *xeros* (dry). Drought-tolerant landscaping is one way to conserve residential water use. Due to dry periods and—in Florida—explosive population growth, an increased demand on freshwater resources has resulted in the development of a set of xeriscape principles.

Soil

Growing things start with the soil—the foundation for successful gardening. Soil, the upper layer of the earth's surface in which the roots of plants grow, is made up of organic material, minerals, water, air, and tiny living forms. In order to be an intelligent and successful gardener, you need to have a basic understanding of soil composition.

Add organic materials to firm sand or loosen clay, to increase water-holding capacity in sand or allow water to drain from clay. Organic materials incorporate nutrients and help soil hold them so that they are available for the roots of plants. They also change the pH of your soil to suit the plants and make cultivation easier.

Soil Vocabulary

Being familiar with a few terms will help you manage your soil.

Soil aeration. This is the process of loosening the soil by mechanical means in order to increase porosity to water and air. The roots of plants can't live without adequate oxygen.

Soil amendment. This means improving soil for better drainage, moisture retention, and aeration by adding chemicals, minerals, organic matter, or other fillers such as perlite or vermiculite. Organic matter comes from the breakdown of things that were once alive, such as leaves, grass clippings, fruits, and vegetables. The end products of this decomposition are compost and peat moss.

Soil sterilization. This is accomplished by fumigation (heat, chemical, or steam) to free soil of harmful organisms. There are advantages and disadvantages to this procedure because killing bad organisms necessitates destroying good organisms.

Soil testing. This test is a scientific analysis of a soil sample's acidity or alkalinity. It also checks for the presence of organisms and examines the texture and the nutrient content in order to gauge the soil's suitability for certain uses or to determine the adjustment necessary to adapt it to a particular use.

Taking a soil sample is as important as testing it. Use a clean trowel and clean plastic bags, and do not touch the soil with your hands. Gather a relatively dry sample from the surface of several areas that have not been recently fertilized. Take a core that is one-half inch across and six inches deep in each area. Label cores according to their location in the garden. Then take your samples to a city beautification department, a university extension service, or any of the extension service's county agriculture centers for a free soil evaluation. Or you may buy a kit and do the test yourself.

Kinds of Soil

Some areas have peat and some have clay, but most seacoast gardens have sandy, alkaline soil. Therefore, nearly all soil has to be amended before plants can thrive.

Soil types are referred to as sand, silt, loam, peat, muck, humus, and clay. Sandy soil is composed of large, loose particles, which dry out readily. It is usually low in nutrients. These problems of sandy soil are compounded in coastal areas by the presence of salts not only in the soil but also in the water and air. Clay soil is just the opposite. It is dense, packed into a very fine texture, has no room for air, and drains poorly. Silt, peat, and loam fall somewhere between sand and clay and contain varying amounts of organic material. Loam implies a well-balanced garden soil that contains part clay, part sand, and part organic materials. Peat refers to decayed organic plant matter from ancient swamps and is used for soil improvement. It is dark in color and has to be combined with other materials for proper drainage and to be suitable as a growing medium. Humus also means decomposed organic matter. Muck is mud of undefined content.

Amending Soil

Few soils are ideal for gardening in their natural state. Gardeners strive for a soil that will hold nutrients well and that is loose enough to drain well but able to hold enough moisture to satisfy the plant's demands. Most soils can be improved. The best remedy is to add the correct amounts of spongy organic materials—compost, peat moss, manures—depending upon the basic soil type. It is almost impossible to work too much humus into sandy soil. The consistency is right when you can insert your spade with little effort. Soil has to be loose enough to allow oxygen to enter and roots to penetrate but firm enough to hold plants securely.

Sandy and clay soils require the constant addition of organic matter to grow plants successfully. Organic matter added to the soil incorporates nutrients, helps loosen clay particles, firms sand particles, supplies air spaces, and adjusts drainage. A general formula for good growing soil is one-third sand, one-third peat, and one-third compost or other organic material.

Soil pH

It's necessary to understand soil reaction. Soils can be acid, alkaline, or neutral. Acidity and alkalinity are measured on the pH scale, a scale symbol that runs from 0 to 14. A pH of 7.0 is neutral. Below 7 measures acidity, above 7 alkalinity. Some plants thrive best in acidic soils, some prefer alkaline, while most others are able to adapt to a rather wide range (5.5 to 7.5). In general, if the pH drops below 5 or is higher than 7.5, special problems develop. Plants that grow best in acid soils include azalea, camellia, croton, dogwood, gardenia, hibiscus, holly, and magnolia. In contrast, cactus, coontie, sea grape, many succulents, wedelia, yucca, and a number of palms thrive in alkaline soil. Most vegetables do best in soil with a pH of 6 to 7.

The practical way to get an idea of the pH of your soil is to observe plants in the area and read nature's own signs. If the soil is loose and colorless and nothing much is growing in the area except pine trees, cacti, and weeds, you can be pretty sure the soil is alkaline and of poor quality. On the other hand, if the soil appears dark, has a medium-coarse texture, and grows lush and healthy plants, then you can guess that you have a good mixture of acid/alkaline soil. If the soil appears dark and has fat earthworms in it, you probably have acidic soil. Generally speaking, the darker the soil, the richer it is in organic matter. The more organic matter your soil contains, the greater its moisture-retention capacity. The more sand your soil contains, the less its moisture-retention capacity. Strive for a happy medium.

There are a number of ways to raise or lower the pH of soil besides adding organic materials. Soil can be removed from the area and replaced with more suitable soil. Wettable sulfur can be used to acidify soil, or an acid-forming fertilizer can be applied. After applying, immediately wash the sulfur in. Lime or dolomite is used to increase pH when the soil is too acid. After applying any of the above, your soil should be tested because it is sometimes rather difficult to get just the right balance. A small testing gauge for home use is available.

Soil pH is very important because it influences properties that affect growth of plants. These properties may be microorganisms, nutrients, leaching, or contact with noxious materials. But pH alone is not an indication of fertility (successful growth and production). Besides the correct pH, soil must have the capacity to supply nutrients in proper amounts for plant growth (adequate nitrogen, phosphorus, and potassium, plus minor trace elements such as iron, copper, manganese, boron, and zinc.) Other factors that influence fertility are nutrient content, organic matter, and drainage. Without proper drainage air cannot reach the roots.

If you plan to use compost soil for houseplants, it should be sterilized. Lightly moisten it, mix well, place in a flat pan with sides no higher than four inches, cover with foil, and bake in a kitchen oven at two hundred degrees for thirty minutes. The soil will have an unpleasant odor, so be prepared to take the pan outdoors immediately after baking. Cool and place in plastic bags.

COMPOST

Because seacoast soils are generally low in organic matter, it's necessary to incorporate material into the soil to improve its fertility and ability to hold moisture. The most economical and ecological way to do this is by composting.

Composting is an important way to use nature as a guide to gardening. Recycling began with composting, which has been nature's method from the beginning.

Definition of Compost

Compost is a homogenous organic material that results from the decomposition of various types of plant and animal refuse. The final product is sometimes referred to as humus. In order to achieve satisfactory decomposition it is necessary to have moisture, air (oxygen), microorganisms, organic materials, and warmth.

Advantages of Making and Using Compost

Composting is not only recycling at its best but also an essential part of successful gardening. It saves time and money and assures that a convenient supply of soil-amending material is on hand at all times. Unlike most fertilizers, the nutrient content of compost is released to plants gradually so that the soil is improved over a long period of time.

Locations for Composting

There are a number of ways to store your compost so that it won't be offensive or unsightly: a haystack pile, a hole dug in the ground, a bin, commercial containers, a large garbage can, or a plastic bag. The type of enclosure you choose will depend on the amount of compost you can use and the space available. Make the pile big enough to heat rapidly and retain heat and moisture but not so large that you can't turn it with ease. Four feet across and three feet in depth is a practical size. Turning simply means aerating, stirring, and mixing.

Bins can be constructed from concrete blocks, bricks, crossties, boards, or wire. Some bins have concrete floors, while others are placed directly on the ground. It is best to choose an area in the shade, protected from the wind, on ground that will drain well and that is near a water hose. Sunlight kills microorganisms and dries the pile out too rapidly. If the pile is too dry, it won't heat up. If it is too wet, it will have a bad odor.

How to Compost

Whatever method you choose for composting, keep in mind that the end product is the same—decomposition. The method is as simple as making a casserole: loosely layering over and over again. Heat, necessary for decomposition, is produced by the quick decay of nitrogen-rich materials. For best results, all ingredients should have a fine consistency—shredded or chopped—in lightly applied layers to allow oxygen throughout the pile. The pile should be kept moist at all times but not soggy.

Never dump leaves or grass clippings into a pile. Instead, scatter them evenly over the top. Some gardeners construct a wire screen through which the mature compost is sifted before using. Potting soil requires a finer screen than soil used in the garden.

Be selective about what you put in your compost pile. Use only refuse that will break down easily. Avoid things like sticks, tough cornstalks, cones, bamboo stalks, and magnolia leaves. Also, large leaves such as maple, sycamore, and palm have a tendency to mat together so water can't seep through. Shred this material before adding it to the pile. To avoid killing earthworms and other beneficial organisms, never compost grass clippings right after they have been treated with pesticides or herbicides.

Serious gardeners keep several compost piles in order to have soil in various stages of decomposition: mature soil, completely decomposed; mulch soil, partially decomposed; and their most recent collection. The amount of maturity, or richness, of the soil can be determined by the dark color, the blended texture, the size of earthworms, and an earthy smell.

Earthworms are a gardener's best friend. They are an important component of a compost pile and useful in the garden soil too. Earthworms multiply rapidly while continually aerating and fertilizing your soil or compost. If your garden doesn't have a good supply, it is possible to buy a few starters from a worm farm.

Start your compost with a six-inch layer made up of items such as these: grass clippings, leaves, manures, wood ashes (potash), hay, straw, pine needles, shrubbery clippings, spent garden plants (peas, beans, tomatoes), peat moss, seaweed, and kitchen refuse such as fruits, vegetables, potato and banana peels, lettuce, cabbage, carrot tops, tea and coffee grounds, and crushed eggshells. Don't use any cooked or greasy materials because they will interfere with the microbiological action and cause odors.

Ideally, the second layer should be a half-inch or so of animal manure or a sprinkling of nitrogen-rich fertilizer. Here is the University of Florida Extension Service recommendation: for a three-by-three-foot area, allow about one foot of organic material to build up. Then sprinkle seven pounds of 6-6-6 fertilizer over the pile.

Alternate layers of organic refuse, manures and/or commercial fertilizer, peat, and topsoil. You should include some green materials such as leaves or grass clippings for the chlorophyll content, which supplies heat and helps repress odors. A light covering of topsoil between layers of organic materials is another way to prevent odors. Also, turning and moistening the pile provides proper aeration that speeds up the decaying process, which helps keep the pile odor-free. If you abide by these instructions, there should never be an unpleasant odor from your compost pile.

Maintaining Your Compost Pile

A pitchfork has proven to be the most convenient tool for turning compost. Proper turning of the pile is important. You don't want to turn it so often that you allow heat to escape, but you must aerate often enough to supply oxygen so that bacteria can do their work. If your compost is clumped and gooey, it's probably too wet and needs more air.

If you place your compost in a hole about four feet square by two to three feet deep, save the soil from the hole for layering. When you need more soil for layering, simply enlarge the hole. If the center of the pile is a little lower than the sides (dish-shaped), it will help water drain inward rather than off the pile. A sheet of plastic can be placed over the pile to hold moisture and heat and to hasten composition. Remove the plastic when the pile has started to heat, and mix the center material with the outside material. If you're using a bin, cover it with a lid.

The length of time necessary for complete breakdown depends on conditions such as heat, cold, rain, worms, the nature of materials used, and the frequency of turning. Plant material should decompose into good soil in two to five months.

When only a small amount of soil is needed, the garbage can or plastic bag method is recommended. Layer the compost ingredients in the container and sprinkle with fertilizer. Add enough water to moisten well, but not saturate, and put the lid on or tie the bag tightly. Turn the bag, or roll the can around on its side, from time to time. You should have complete breakdown in about eight weeks.

When you have established your compost production, it's a good idea to have a soil test to determine just what kind of soil you're turning out. The pH will indicate the alkalinity or the acidity. Following the instructions in this chapter should produce soil on the acid side, which is what is needed most often in seacoast gardens in order for plants to thrive. If you want to raise or lower the pH of your compost soil, use additives as described in section on soil.

Some gardeners use sheet composting, which involves spreading the organic materials in layers about four inches deep over the surface of the entire garden. This organic material is then tilled under several weeks before planting time.

Commercial compost activators are available. They contain high concentrations of selected microorganisms that accelerate decomposition when your compost pile seems to need a boost.

Seaweed—kelp—is a natural organic fertilizer and can be added to compost in layers. Primitive humans discovered that livestock fed on seaweed thrived, and the Greeks, Chinese, and Vikings applied it to the soil. A remarkable soil conditioner, seaweed acts as a binder for soil particles. It contains moderate amounts of nitrogen and huge amounts of potassium. In decomposition, it produces plant hormones that have an important effect on root development and general growth. Trace elements in seaweed help guard against diseases and insects and increase the germination of seeds. Seaweed also seems to stimulate blossom and fruit development. Seacoast gardeners should gather seaweed from the beach after it is somewhat dry. Spread it out, rinse well with the garden hose to remove some of the salt, and then add it to a compost pile.

MULCH

Mulch is a layer of material, preferably organic matter, that is placed on the soil surface to conserve moisture, help prevent erosion, help keep roots cool in summer and warm in winter, discourage weed growth, supply more organic matter to the soil, and reduce maintenance. It helps keep flowers, fruits, and vegetables clean and insect-free because it covers the dirt. Mulches can also add color and texture and give the overall landscape a tidy appearance. Mulches are used under and around trees, shrubs, flowers, and vegetables as well as for garden paths.

Kinds of Mulch

There are two kinds of mulch: organic (from plants and animals) and inorganic (stones, gravel, plastic). Organic mulch eventually decomposes into compost and then into rich soil called humus, adding nutrients to plants. When organic mulch decomposes, fresh mulch should then be applied.

Organic. Materials that can be used as mulch are the same as those listed in the instructions for composting, except for sawdust. Sawdust is high in carbohydrates but low in nitrogen. When sawdust decomposes, it takes nitrogen from the soil instead of supplying it. Therefore, when using sawdust as mulch, add one or two cups of fertilizer high in nitrogen for each bushel of sawdust.

Fresh grass clippings should not be used alone because they mildew and, in the decomposition process, generate tremendous amounts of heat that can damage root systems. However, grass clippings are excellent to mix in your compost pile with other ingredients. The heat speeds up breakdown of compost, and the green adds chlorophyll.

Plastic. Sheets of plastic are not recommended for general garden mulch. When plastic is used, holes should be punched in it and organic mulch put over the top to reduce heat absorption and improve the appearance.

Bark. Tree bark (pine, cypress) mulches are effective in enhancing the landscape. Bark can be successfully used for improving soil mix due to its many gradations in particle size, the species from which it came, and the variable treatment given to it before marketing. Bark adds organic matter to the soil, controls erosion, and protects roots from cold and heat. There are differences in color, texture, size of particles, weight, and water-absorbing abilities that give the landscaper a wide latitude in producing special effects. The larger chunks are referred to as nuggets, the smaller chunks as mini-nuggets, and the finer material as shredded bark. It is best to use a layer of shredded bark, or plastic, under nuggets. Weeds that come up through nuggets can be difficult to remove.

Management of Mulch

As a rule, mulch should be about three inches in depth—no deeper than four inches—and kept at that level. If mulch gets low, roots will have a tendency to grow into it instead of downward. In order to avoid crown and stem rotting and insect invasion, don't pile the mulch against trunks and lower limbs. Be sure to leave an open space six inches to a foot around the trunk.

It's best to weed, fertilize, and water well before applying mulch. Weeds that come through can be pulled by hand. Weeds are easier to pull when the soil is damp.

Alternatives for Mulch

Groundcovers and cover crops—called green manure—are used for purposes similar to compost and mulch. They have vigorous growing habits and generally shade the ground well so weeds are kept at a minimum. High in nitrogen, cover crops are tilled under at the end of their season, thus greatly enriching the soil.

Specific Ways to Use Mulch

When planting in hills and rows, mulch heavily between the hills, and alternate the planting between the hills and vales each year. This continually enriches the soil and raises the soil level to promote good drainage.

In areas where you don't turn mulch under—as in rose beds—add fresh mulch as necessary but take care not to disturb the roots of plants. The roots of rose bushes grow in a shallow spreading pattern. If there's any sign of insect invasion, dust an insecticide around the bushes before applying new mulch.

Mulches are especially helpful for plants that need warm soil such as melons, beans, eggplant, okra, and tomatoes. They are also helpful for tender plants and those with roots that grow near the surface—particularly azaleas and roses.

Like compost, mulch makes gardening easier and the garden healthier, more productive, and more attractive.

FERTILIZER

Given enough water and sunshine, soils that are more fertile produce better than poor soils do. But any soil can lose its nutrients through erosion, leaching, and growing crops, which makes it necessary to re-build with supplements. Therefore, to grow plants in any soil, gardeners should understand supplements—commercial and organic fertilizers.

Types of Fertilizers

We think in terms of two kinds of fertilizers, chemical and organic. Each may lack minor elements that the other may supply. There are advantages to using either type, but combining the two often works out best to keep the seacoast garden healthy and beautiful.

Chemical (commercial) fertilizers. These fertilizers are man-made of major elements needed by plants. When time is of the essence, chemical fertilizers work faster. The slow release of organics is desirable in sandy soil, but slow-release chemical fertilizers are also available.

Slow release means release of nutrients in regulated amounts. Slow-release fertilizers—granular or pellet—are coated with some material through which water slowly penetrates to release the soluble contents. This type is applied less frequently than regular fertilizers.

Organic (natural) fertilizers. These are derived from some form of organic matter—animals, plants, manures, or composted material. Organics don't leach out of the ground as rapidly as commercial fertilizers do because, before the nitrogen can be converted to plant availability, they require a slow breakdown by microorganisms. Warm temperatures are necessary for decomposition because microorganisms fail to act during cold weather.

Organic fertilizers, also available from supply stores, are more expensive than chemical fertilizers. Organics can contain varying percentages of organic materials and may be natural or synthetic. Urea is an example of a synthetic organic nitrogen because chemically it contains the element carbon. With chemical fertilizers, burning of roots or foliage is a common hazard, but organic fertilizers won't burn if you happen to overfertilize. However, if you are depending on organics for your major fertilizer, it may be necessary to add trace elements in chemical form.

Nutrients Needed by Plants

Do you simply apply plant food to your plants, or do you know what's in that bag of fertilizer?

The three most important nutrients for plant development are indicated by the three analysis numbers found on the fertilizer bags. These three primary nutrients are nitrogen (N), phosphorus (P), and potassium (K). The numbers always appear in the same sequence. In addition to these three, some of the more expensive fertilizers contain the secondary nutrients sulfur, calcium, and magnesium. The remaining trace elements are iron, copper, boron, molybdenum, manganese, and zinc. These are called trace or micronutrients because a plant needs very small quantities of them.

The rest of the contents in the bag of fertilizer are fillers such as sand, peat, manures, and sludge, which may or may not have some value as a source of plant nutrients. Beware of discount fertilizers. You may get more sand, pebbles, or sawdust than nutrients. Florida law requires that an analysis be displayed on every bag of fertilizer sold.

Fertilizer analysis shows the percentages of ingredients by weight. For instance, the numbers on packages of fertilizer, such as 6-6-6 or 10-6-4, indicate percentages of nitrogen, phosphorus, and potassium (N, P, K) by weight. For example, in a bag of 6-6-6, the first 6—for nitrogen—means 6 percent by weight, or six pounds of nitrogen for each one hundred pounds of fertilizer. The same is true of the 6 for phosphorus and the 6 for potassium. This totals eighteen pounds of major nutrients, so you get eighteen pounds of major nutrients per one hundred pounds of fertilizer. The other eighty-two pounds are filler material.

Fillers make the plant food easier to spread. The filler material may also contain conditioners that help keep the fertilizer from hardening in the bag.

Plants need more nitrogen than any other nutrient, which creates a particular problem in sandy soils that leach rapidly. Nitrogen is the principal promoter of blade, leaf, and stem growth. Important for chlorophyll production, it gives plants their vibrant green color. Lacking nitrogen, the plant loses this color, becomes pale and yellow, produces weak growth, and yields inferior flowers and fruit. If applied in amounts too large, nitrogen may burn; if applied too often, it may cause excessive foliage growth, fewer flowers, and consequently less fruit.

The second major nutrient, phosphorus, promotes the development of roots and the maturity of roots, stems, and blossoms. Phosphorus is made from phosphate ore; therefore, it remains in the soil and becomes available to plants over a period of time.

Potassium, the third major nutrient in fertilizer, is potash ore, or wood ashes. It can be used in its original form. Potassium helps make stems and roots strong and crisp, increases resistance to drought stress, improves winter hardiness, and contributes to overall health.

All three of these nutrients are important for disease resistance. When combined in commercial fertilizer, they are in a form that makes them available to plants.

Fertilizer Balance

Fertilizers are classed as complete, balanced, unbalanced, or complete unbalanced. If a fertilizer mix contains all three of the major plant nutrients, it is called a complete fertilizer. When only one or two are present, it is referred to as incomplete. A balanced fertilizer contains all three major nutrients in equal amounts (6-6-6, 8-8-8, 20-20-20). A complete unbalanced fertilizer contains all three major nutrients, but each is not present in equal amounts (10-6-4, 10-10-5).

Ideally, a soil test should be made so that you will know your soil content. (See the section on soil.) However, in general a complete balanced fertilizer should be used to take care of any possible deficiency of the three major nutrient elements.

When to Fertilize

Fertilize most plants only when they are actively growing, during spring and summer into a warm fall. Gradually decrease the amounts and frequency of application in the fall. Fall fertilizers should be low in nitrogen. Stop completely during winter when plants are dormant. Gradually resume feeding in the early spring. Flowering trees and shrubs should not be fed while in bloom. There are, of course, exceptions and variables concerning the fertilization of plants that must be learned depending upon the individual plant.

How to Fertilize

There are several ways to apply fertilizer.

On the ground. Water-soluble fertilizers, mixed with water before applying, are available in tablet, powder, or liquid form. Slow-release fertilizers are usually in the form of granules and are applied only every few months because the nutrients are released gradually with each watering. Granules are mixed into the surface of the soil, then watered.

The hole, or punch-bar, method is no longer recommended for fertilizing trees. Surface applications are thought to be more effective because most roots are in the upper foot of soil. Surface applications should be started from two to three feet from the trunk and extending out a little beyond the drip line.

Avoid overfertilizing. It's better to use small amounts more often than heavy applications less often.

On the leaves. Foliar feeding is applied by spraying the leaves with a product that is soluble in water or a liquid that is added to water. This type is especially useful on any plant requiring immediate attention. Sometimes a plant is unable to absorb fertilizer through its roots but will respond immediately to fertilizer sprayed on its leaves. It is best not to use foliar feeding when plants are dry or in hot sunshine because the leaves may absorb the spray too quickly and become scorched. When spraying plants with fuzzy leaves, use a fine mist and be sure the solution is a little warmer than room temperature.

Deficiencies

After some gardening experience you will be able to recognize the more obvious nutritional deficiencies of your plants. Generally, a deficiency of any of the main nutrients will make its presence known in the older foliage rather than the new. Deficiency signs can be inconsistent. They depend on the type of plant, and identification can become complicated. For example, lack of magnesium, zinc, manganese, and iron all show up as yellowing between the stem and veins on the leaves while the veins remain green. Deficiency of iron, especially for acid-loving plants, is the most common minor element problem found in Florida's sandy soils. It's best to take some leaves to your favorite nursery for proper identification of any deficiency.

Lack of calcium and phosphorus can be corrected by using bone meal, which is an additive high in both. Superphosphate (0-20-0) is readily available phosphate that is used when more is needed for development of roots, stems, and blossoms.

Fertilizer Types

Gardening has been made easier by the manufacture of special fertilizer blends that are designed to meet the particular needs of specific plants. Labels may read *Camellia-Azalea, Citrus Special, Rose Special, Tomato Special, Palm and Ixora, Bed Mix,* or *Weed-and-Feed;* or they may advertise a product that is high in phosphorus and potassium to promote flowering (4-11-11). Weed-and-feed fertilizers contain herbicides and should be used with caution. Trees and shrubs can take up the herbicide through their roots and be severely damaged or killed.

Fertilizers labeled *organic* can contain varying percentages of organic materials, which may be natural or synthetic.

Some fertilizers contain pesticides. Read the labels carefully and use only on plants for which they are specifically recommended.

Healthy soil is the key to successful gardening. Most soils require supplements to adequately nourish plants. Consult your county agent or favorite nursery for specific advice.

PROPAGATION

Propagation is the word used for the reproduction of plants. There are a number of ways that this can be accomplished: from seeds, stems, roots, leaves, budding, grafting, and tissue culture. The method will vary with the type of plant.

The average home gardener doesn't need to propagate plants because so many are available as plantlets. However, one of the most rewarding things about gardening is creating something out of nothing and watching it grow and develop.

Propagation from Seeds

Growing plants from seeds is easy. Always buy quality seeds, and carry out the instructions on the package. Few old seeds will germinate, so pay close attention to dates on packages. Seeds with hard shells will remain viable up to one year, but many others won't germinate if they have been allowed to dry out. When stored correctly, most flower and vegetable seeds will last from the time they are harvested until the next planting season. Store seeds in a refrigerator—not in the freezer—in a closed, dry container.

Seeds from many kinds of plants will reproduce true to type, but most hybrids will not. If these hybrid seeds should sprout, chances are the fruit or flowers of the resulting plants will be inferior. Plants that naturally self-pollinate will reproduce true to type, but plants that cross-pollinate may produce offspring different from the parent.

Most garden seeds germinate at soil temperatures between seventy and eighty degrees. To get a head start, plant in flats or pots indoors where you can keep the soil warm. Follow instructions on the seed packet, water well, and cover with a piece of clear plastic. As soon as seeds begin to sprout, remove the plastic and expose the plantlets to sunlight if they are plants that normally grow in full sun. When the young sprouts have a pair of fully developed leaves, eliminate the weaker sprouts and transplant the stronger ones into small pots. Place in partial shade. When roots begin to show at the bottom of the pots, it is time to set the seedlings out in the garden or into larger pots.

Propagation from Cuttings

A cutting is a portion of a plant cut from a parent plant for the purpose of growing roots and leaves to produce a new plant. There are stem cuttings, leaf cuttings, and root cuttings.

Stem cuttings. There are three kinds of stem cuttings: softwood, semi-hardwood, and hardwood.

Softwood stem cuttings are taken, with leaves attached, from young, half-hardened spring growth from plants such as aralia, boxwood, crape myrtle, Chinese evergreen, coleus, dieffenbachia, dracaena, hibiscus, impatiens, jasmine, magnolia, monstera, oleander, peperomia, rubber, schef-flera, shrimp, and zebra. The wood must be flexible but mature enough to make a clean break when bent sharply.

Cuttings from plants with fleshy stems or milky sap should be set aside until the sap dries and hardens before planting. This type of plant includes geranium, jade, poinsettia, Christmas cactus, crown-of-thorns, and succulents.

Semi-hardwood cuttings differ from softwood cuttings only in maturity of the wood—six to nine weeks after a flush of growth when the wood is partially matured. Anytime is good from mid-spring to mid-fall in Florida for azalea, bougainvillea, camellia, croton, gardenia, geranium, hibiscus, holly, honeysuckle, hydrangea, juniper, pittosporum, and pyracantha. Leave only two or three leaves at the top.

Hardwood cuttings are best taken in the fall from the mature wood of crape myrtle, fig, grape, juniper, oleander, spirea, and wisteria.

Leaf cuttings. The two kinds of leaf cuttings are leaf-blade cuttings and leaf-stalk cuttings.

Leaf-blade cuttings are simply a piece of leaf cut off and planted, top side up. The new plants actually sprout from the leaf blade. Examples are sansevieria, Rex begonia, and kalanchoe.

Leaf-stalk cuttings are leaves removed with some stem still attached. The stems of leaf-stalk cuttings are dipped in rooting hormone and buried in soil to the base of the leaf. The roots and shoots arise from the base of the leaf stalk. Examples are African violets, begonias, echeveria, jade, and peperomia.

Root cuttings. Some plants such as croton, impatiens, hibiscus, ivy, begonia, Swedish ivy, coleus, philodendron, pothos, gardenia, and oleander can be rooted simply by placing cuttings in a glass of water. After tiny roots develop they can be planted in potting soil. When rooting in water, remove leaves from the lower part of stem so no foliage falls below the water level. Soil and foliage in the water will decay, produce a bad odor, and cause the cuttings to die. Replenish the water supply as it is consumed, and completely change it as it becomes cloudy. Rainwater is preferred to tap water. For rooting, a bright location out of direct sunlight is best.

How to Make a Cutting

When taking any kind of cutting, make a clean cut about one-half inch below a node (joint) with a sharp knife or clippers. Avoid crushing the stem. The cutting tool should be as clean as possible. A solution of liquid bleach can be used to sterilize tools.

How to Plant a Cutting

To plant a cutting, dip the cut end about one inch into a rooting hormone. In potting soil, preferably sterile, which is loose and will drain well, make a hole with a stick and gently insert several inches of the end of the cutting so that the hormone is not brushed off. Firm the soil so that the cutting remains upright. Water gently and keep the soil moist, but not wet, until your plant is growing well. Cuttings must not be allowed to wilt before or after planting except those with fleshy stems or milky sap.

To retain moisture in the soil and keep humidity at an even level, place a plastic bag over the top of the pot so that it clears the cutting by several inches. Tuck the bag snugly around the sides of the pot. A stick may be placed in the center of the pot to serve as a tent pole.

Sand is a favorite for rooting cuttings. A mixture of sand and peat moss, sand and vermiculite, perlite and peat moss, or any mixture that ensures good drainage and aeration can be used.

Other Methods of Propagation

There are several other methods of propagating plants.

Division of root ball. This is a method of dividing many perennials whose root systems have become too large. Simply dig up the plant, leaving a firm root ball. Cut the foliage back to about four inches tall and remove all dead leaves. Then cut the clump into pieces with a sharp spade or knife, and replant the pieces. The number of pieces depends on the size of the root ball that you are dividing. The average approach is to cut the root ball into fourths. Fertilize lightly and keep well watered. Fall or early spring are the best times for this procedure. Examples of plants that benefit from this method are bamboo, black-eyed Susan, day lily, liriope, mondo grass, and Shasta daisy.

Air layering. This easy technique for propagating many landscape plants allows you to gain a large transplant that might otherwise take several years to reach a similar size (see figure 1). The method is particularly useful for salvaging flourishing tops of plants that have become too leggy. At the same time, the size of the parent plant becomes fuller and more beautiful. The ideal time to do air layering is in the spring on the previous season's growth.

To air-layer you need a sharp knife, wet sphagnum moss, rooting hormone, string, and plastic wrap. Soak the moss overnight in a solution containing a soluble or liquid balanced fertilizer.

If possible, choose a branch that has firm, mature wood and is growing upright. Make a wound by girdling the branch—removing a narrow ring of bark. Make two cuts about one inch apart just below a leaf stalk or joint and carefully remove the ring of bark between the cuts. Coat the area with a hormone rooting powder, using a little brush.

Air layering induces root development on the branch of a plant by moving nutrients—taken in by foliage—downward to the air-layer site. Where the wound interrupts this flow, the materials accumulate and latent roots form.

Squeeze a handful of the soaked sphagnum moss until it is only slightly moist, make a pancake, and wrap it snugly around the cut area. Wrap a ten inch by ten inch piece of clear plastic around the moss, overlapping the edges, and tie (or tape) it firmly at each end. Don't ever unwrap the plastic to check on the rooting progress. The new roots will grow into this moss and can be seen through the plastic as they develop. The ties should be tight so the moisture will be retained in the moss. If the moss dries out, the roots won't develop properly. Keep the mother plant well watered and spray the foliage every few days.

The length of time for root development beneath the plastic varies

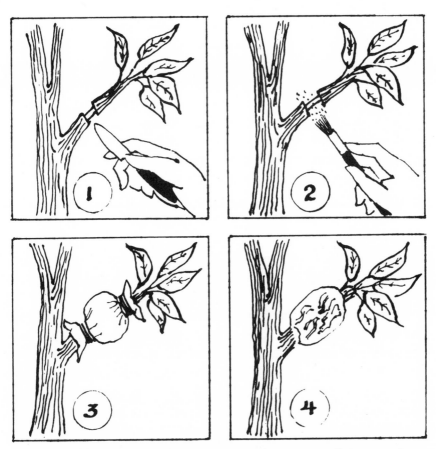

Figure 1. Air layering. 1. Using a sharp knife, make a girdling wound, removing a narrow ring of bark on a mature, firm branch. 2. Dust the wound with hormone rooting powder. 3. Make a pancake of moist sphagnum moss and wrap it around the cut area. Cover the moss with clear plastic and tie securely. 4. Check in a few weeks to see whether roots are growing in the moss. If so, the new plant is ready to be removed from the mother and planted.

with type of plant and weather conditions. Wait for a strong root system to form. When you can plainly see strong roots growing in the moss, you can separate your new plant from its mother. Cut the stem immediately below the new roots, remove the plastic, and your new plant is ready to be planted. The bare stem left on the mother plant below the air layer will grow new terminal leaves very soon.

Air layering is not satisfactory for all shrubbery. Some plants that lend themselves to air layering are crotons, camellias, gardenias, hibiscus, ixora, viburnum, azaleas, and certain fruit trees.

Cane plants. A number of cane plants can be grown by burying stem sections. These plants, which have jointed stems, include dieffenbachia, dracaena, bamboo, and some gingers. Cut stems into small sections of one or two leaf joints and lay them horizontally, half submerged in soil. A new leaf will appear at an old leaf joint, with more leaves appearing as roots develop.

Aerial plantlets. Plants such as strawberry, spider, begonia, iris, and walking iris send off shoots from the parent plant that produce aerial plantlets. These babies can be planted while still connected to their mothers and cut loose after they develop their own solid root system, or they can be cut loose and the tiny air roots imbedded in soil to grow on their own.

Cuttings made from roots. These cuttings are usually taken in late fall or very early spring from two- to three-year-old stock plants such as clerodendrum, oak-leaf hydrangea, plumbago, wisteria, and yucca. Pieces of root, pencil-thick or thicker, are cut into short lengths and placed horizontally in the rooting soil. They should be covered with about one-half inch of soil. It isn't necessary to have any part of the plant showing above ground level.

Layering trailing branches. This method is sometimes thought of as natural propagation. Cut off the leaves of a portion of the vine, make a wound on the side that will be down, slightly cover with soil, weigh it down with a brick, and keep it watered. Check on it from time to time by carefully removing some soil off the top. When roots have formed, cut the layered section from the mother plant and replant.

❀

CHAPTER 2

Control Techniques

GARDEN PESTS

It isn't possible to become a relaxed gardener until you've learned to recognize the most common garden pests and diseases. Gardening should be a leisure activity, and the pleasures involved should not be decreased by insects and other pests and the damage they do.

First, it is essential to recognize environmental ailments that often have symptoms similar to disease and insect damage. We should try to learn to tell the difference and recognize the cause. For example, leaf scorch and fungi are common ailments prevalent in hot, humid Florida. The cause of burned, wilted leaves when temperatures are above ninety degrees is obvious. Some things can appear to be disease and insect damage but are problems brought on by living conditions, such as too little moisture, too much moisture, too great a variation in watering, modern industrial pollutants, overfertilization, and a lack of soil nutrients.

Actually, the most troublesome pests are relatively few in number, and if we learn to recognize them, it's easy to take combative steps. Early recognition is of the utmost importance, followed by professional advice when an insecticide is indicated.

Types of Insects

There are three ways that pests damage plants: (1) chewing, (2) piercing and sucking, and (3) boring or internal feeding.

Insects with chewing mouth parts. Insects that feed on foliage and other plant parts by biting and swallowing portions of the plant leave holes or ragged edges. Chewers include caterpillars, beetles, grasshoppers, crickets, katydids, grubs, and worms. They eat leaves, flowers, stems, or roots.

Insects with piercing and sucking mouth parts. These insects include scales, aphids, whiteflies, mealybugs, stink bugs, leafhoppers, and chinch bugs. This type simply pierces plant tissue and sucks out the juices. Damage appears as withered and curled leaves or as small spots on leaves and stems. Fruit attacked by piercing-sucking insects will be deformed or wilted.

Insects that bore into plants. Boring-mining insects tunnel into plant stems, roots, bark, or fruit. At the first signs of their work, leaves appear curled and brown. The death of an entire limb follows. Many of these are the larvae stage of beetles. Leaf miners belong to this group and are especially damaging.

Stages of an Insect's Life

Most insects pass through several stages in their development. Some hatch from eggs deposited on or near their food supply. Some hatch within the female's body, others produce nymphs, and still others go through larval stages. Most adult stages have wings, but a few do not. The larva of a moth or a butterfly is called a caterpillar, the larva of a beetle is called a grub, and the larva of a fly is known as a maggot. Therefore, timing of control must match the most susceptible stage.

Specific Pests

Thrips are one of the pests most destructive of flowers. These insects are minute, agile, winged, and have rasping-sucking mouth parts. Unlike most other insects, they prefer plants that are mature, and they feed between leaves and petals, where they are sheltered from insecticide spray. Watch closely for tiny black specks moving about on petals of roses, mums, daisies, and glads. They also like beans, onions, citrus, pears, and greenhouse plants.

Aphids are also pests with sucking mouth parts that attack young, tender growth. They cause new buds to be deformed and leaves to curl and twist. Aphids are small and vary in color but can usually be seen best as lime-green clusters smothering new growth and buds of plants such as hibiscus. They secrete a sweet, sticky sap that attracts ants and is a growing medium for a fungus called sooty mold. Aphids multiply rapidly.

Whitefly adults, which are about one-sixteenth of an inch long, are white and resemble tiny moths. The nymphs are found on the undersides of leaves and cause damage by sucking juices. They deposit a sticky substance on leaves and fruit. Sooty mold grows on this substance, causing a black coating that prevents sunlight from reaching the surface of the leaves. Unfortunately, the average gardener is usually unaware of their presence until they hatch out, are disturbed, and swarm about the plant. Whiteflies especially enjoy citrus, gardenia, camellia, and ligustrum. Peak broods appear as soon as warm weather arrives, and they may hang around until fall. It's very important that these pests are controlled early. Repeated sprayings with the correct insecticide are necessary. Washing the foliage with a strong stream from a hose or spraying with a solution of one tablespoon of detergent per gallon of water will help.

Spider mites (red spiders), which feed on the undersides of leaves, are so small that the home gardener often doesn't realize their presence until the damage is severe. When plants are heavily infested, the foliage turns bronze and fine webbing appears. Spider mites are most often found on conifers such as cedar, juniper, and Italian cypress. These pests have several stages in their cycle—green, yellow, then red. They suck juices from the plant but can be eradicated by repeated sprayings with a special miticide.

Mealybugs, soft-bodied sucking insects covered with a white, powdery material, are easy to see because they resemble tiny bits of cotton. They are also very easy to destroy with alcohol on a cotton swab or by washing with soapy water. Mealybugs are often found in a greenhouse or houseplant environment.

Caterpillars are the larvae of butterflies or moths. By chewing, they work fast to devour foliage and petals. They are easy to see and should be picked off by hand when they first appear.

Grasshoppers can consume large quantities of foliage. The small black ones that suddenly hatch out in your garden will grow into very large, yellow-orange adults, so don't delay your attack. Hand picking at the first onset is the best solution. When this type of grasshopper reaches maturity, they are very difficult to kill with an insecticide spray.

Leafminer adults are rarely seen because they are very small flies. They lay their eggs in clusters on the undersides of leaves. Their larvae are translucent maggots found in winding tunnels in the leaves. Sometimes the tunnels appear as trails, other times as blotches. They especially like the leaves of vegetables and ornamentals.

Katydids, which are green and similar in appearance to green grasshoppers, live in trees, chew leaves, and sing an incessant chorale. I'm told that the chorus is all male, sung for the gratification of females, and accomplished by rubbing the ridges of their angular wings together. (To be successful, all books should contain some sex, and this is it for *Florida Gardening by the Sea*.)

Psocid insects, including book lice and bark lice, spin a gossamer silken web on limbs and tree trunks. Don't be alarmed. They will do no harm. They are minute, chewing creatures known as social insects because they live in family groups of various sizes. All stages are sheltered under a net of silk spun from the mouth glands of adults. They feed on lichens, algae, fungi, and decaying plant and animal matter. They do no damage out of doors, but some relatives found indoors feed on glue, paste, and paper. For aesthetic reasons you can use a strong spray from your garden hose to wash them off tree trunks.

Garden slugs and snails are not insects but are nevertheless garden pests. They are slimy mollusks that are related to one another. Snails have shells; slugs don't. They feed at night in damp, shady places, climbing up plants and eating the foliage, especially of tomatoes. A specific bait that will eradicate them is available.

Lawn Pests

Nematodes are microscopic worms that sting the roots of plants and cause distortions known as root-knots. They can be deadly to many plants. Nematodes are very difficult to eradicate, but there are soil fumigants that are of some value. These worms multiply abundantly and seem to thrive in light, sandy soil. Because root-knots prevent the absorption of water and nutrients, they cause plants to die.

Cicada killers are digger wasps and are in a class by themselves. The very large black and yellow wasps arrive in late July and August and dig two-inch holes in lawns. Tunneling as deep as eight inches, they pile dirt up at the entrance to the hole. Cicada wasps can ravage an entire lawn, leaving mounds of dirt all over the place. This wasp then locates a cicada (a large insect), stings and paralyzes it, and brings it back to the burrow. The killer deposits an egg on the cicada. The wasp larvae feed on the paralyzed, but still living, cicada.

Summarizing Garden Pests

In summary, most garden pests can be controlled with a combination of measures: early recognition of the problem, frequent spraying with a forceful stream from a hose, washing with soapy water, companion planting, hand picking, alcohol swabs on light infestations, or organic and chemical sprays. Insecticides, miticides, and baits are available at garden supply stores along with information about which one is indicated and the proper way to use it. When you buy any of the control products, be sure to read the instructions carefully or consult an authority about the safe and correct way to use each product.

There are any number of ways to zap bugs without chemicals, such as traps, predators, and biological controls (ladybugs, mantids, lacewings, birds, trichogramma wasps, soil beetles, or *Bacillus thuringiensis*). These methods aren't as speedy as chemical methods, but they are safe.

It is also interesting to try new recipes or home remedies. Sprays or dusts made from crushed onions, garlic, hot peppers, aromatic herbs, tomato, citrus peels, and geranium leaves—alone or combined—work quite well if the undersides of leaves are well soaked and the spray process is repeated often enough. A remedy for slugs that has some merit is beer in shallow saucers placed around plants. The beer attracts the pests, who then drown in the liquid. Bright yellow cardboard coated with some sticky material attracts flying insects. Companion planting is also worth a try. See the information on insect control in the vegetable garden section of chapter 4.

The most difficult time of year for insect damage in southern gardens is spring into summer, when warm days approach and new tender growth appears. The key to success is to catch garden pests early.

PRUNING

Pruning is an important but much misunderstood garden art. To enjoy pruning and get satisfactory results, we must know why it's necessary, when to do it, and how to prune each plant. No cut should be made without good reason or a full understanding of its execution.

Why We Prune

We prune to maintain plant health by removing dead, weak, diseased, and insect-infested wood; to control shape, height, and size; and to encourage flowering and fruiting. Plants can also be artistically manipulated to produce special effects. According to nature's plan for survival, pruning a plant stimulates growth. Trimming and grooming your plants will rejuvenate them and give a fresh, beautiful, new appearance.

When to Prune

After you understand pruning and learn the needs of individual plants, you can prune year round. Dead wood can be removed, and most plants can be gently shaped and kept in good condition by doing some snipping at almost any time.

Plants that bleed when cut, such as grapevines, have to be pruned during their dormant period, which is after some cold weather has induced a dormant state.

Spring-flowering shrubs and trees should be pruned as soon after blooming as possible, unless the fruit is ornamental or will be harvested. This gives most of the growing season to produce more shoots for more flowers.

Plants that flower in summer or fall are pruned in the dormant season, before the first flush of growth in the spring. Generally, summer pruning should be avoided because it may remove flowering wood. There are exceptions.

Nonflowering deciduous trees, shrubs, and vines are pruned in winter or before foliage buds swell in spring. It is easier to do in the absence of leaves.

Clipped hedges require a specialized type of pruning and may become a continuous job during the growing season. Unless a formal appearance is desired, it's much better to allow your hedges to keep some semblance of their natural shapes. Formal hedges should be clipped while the new growth is young and tender. The plant should be shaped so that the base is a little wider than the top to allow light to reach the lower leaves.

When to prune freeze-damaged plants has always been difficult for new gardeners to understand. Don't be too hasty in pruning cold-damaged plants such as hibiscus, ginger, schefflera, ixora, citrus, croton, gardenia, hydrangea, poinsettia, and allamanda. The extent of cold damage can't be distinctly determined for several weeks. If you prune too soon, you may cut off live wood. Also, leaves and stems that have been killed by frost give some protection to those not yet damaged.

Keep in mind that pruning stimulates new growth. A warming trend following a freeze will activate new, tender growth. Another freeze will kill this growth, and the plant will most likely not be able to overcome a second shock.

The entire tops of some plants can be killed by cold, but their roots may send up new growth in the spring. Don't destroy the plant until you are positive it is dead.

How to Prune

Tools. Begin with the right tools, and be sure they are sharp and in good working condition. The average gardener needs only four pruning tools. Ordinary scissor-type hand shears that have cutting edges on both blades are fine for branches up to one-fourth of an inch in diameter. Long-handled lopping shears are effective for limbs between three-fourths and one and one-fourth inches thick or for those beyond the reach of hand shears. Hedge shears have long scissor-type blades with shorter handles designed for tender growth. For heavier work a crescent-shaped pruning saw is excellent.

Pruning precautions. The growing layer (cambium) of plants is a thin layer of cells just below the bark. This layer is of vital importance in healing and should not be injured. The most prevalent example of damage to cambium layers is careless use of string trimmers.

When pruning, it is important to make a clean, sharp cut without twisting. There is a growing circle at the base of each limb called the branch collar or bark ridge. Look for this slightly raised area and make your cut just outside it. This growing circle contains cells that grow new bark to cover the wound (see figures 2 and 3).

Think of bark as you do your skin and protect it. Plants are living organisms. Each one is an individual. Pruning shocks them. The more

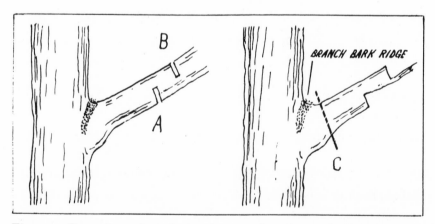

Figure 2. Removing a branch that is more than one and a half inches in diameter. 1. Cut at *A* until the saw binds. 2. Cut at *B* (two to four inches beyond *A*) until the branch falls. 3. Cut at *C*, outside the branch collar.

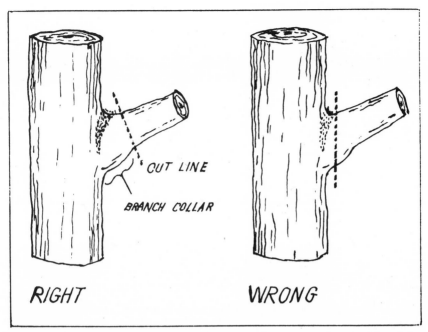

Figure 3. Pruning, right and wrong. Begin the cut on the outside of the branch's bark ridge. The ridge is usually rougher than the surrounding bark and is fairly obvious on most species. Angle the cut so that it ends just above the branch collar. All branches, large and small, should be cut in this manner. Do not cut into the branch collar, and never make a flush cut.

dormant a plant is, the less it will be affected by shock. Sneak up on them while they are resting!

If a branch is diseased or dead, never cut through the bad areas; instead, cut well back into healthy wood.

Pruning paint. Although recent data don't support the practice of applying pruning paint to cuts, it has been my experience with fruit (especially citrus) and shade trees that it seals the wound, keeps out moisture, and helps discourage insects and disease. For better bonding, allow new cuts to dry before applying the paint. Make sure all edges are coated slightly beyond the cut.

Pruning methods. There are two methods of pruning: shearing (as for hedges) and cutting individual branches for thinning.

Where you cut is important. Whatever you do, don't prune branches to leafless stubs. Stubs seldom develop new foliage but decay and attract insects and fungi that will move onto the main trunk. However, stubbing may stimulate the development of water sprouts just below the cut. These rapidly growing shoots will be weak and bear an excessive amount of foliage. They should be selectively removed.

To prune correctly, make a slanting cut just above a bud. This bud will then grow and become the new terminal for the limb. Choose a bud pointing in the general direction that you want the branch to grow. If you wish the branch to grow out, select an outside bud. If you wish more erect or inside growth, choose an inside bud. When thinning, remove excess branches by cutting as far back as you can, flat against the larger branch or trunk.

What you do to a tree in its first few years of life will affect its shape, strength, and even its life span. For the first year or two, a tree needs a maximum of leaf surface to manufacture food for the developing root system. After three or four years, it is time to start cutting off excessive branches and thinning to reduce competition for light, water, and nutrients.

Remember that each species has its own response to, and need for, pruning. In general, when pruning trees, eliminate the lower branches unless there is a particular reason for leaving them intact, such as keeping the natural shape of the tree (for example, holly and Norfolk Island pine). Eliminating the lower branches can remove unsightly foliage, encourage more rapid growth, and allow room for passage beneath them. Pruning may be necessary for special purposes such as controlling the size of a tree that has outgrown its allotted space, is obstructing views, or is shutting out too much sunshine.

Where possible, cut off branches that grow at narrow angles to the trunk and retain those that grow more horizontally. When several branches arise in a tight V-shape, they will most likely be weak and will eventually split as the tree gets larger or limbs get heavy with fruit. Choose one of them to leave and eliminate the others. Removing the lower limbs from trees seems to stimulate growth in the crown and makes them grow tall. There is an old saying about pruning evergreen shrubbery: If you have pruned properly, when you have completed the job, no one will be able to tell that it has just been done.

Specific Plants

Dogwood trees. Remove only dead wood, or you will lose flowers and berries. Runaway limbs can be removed, if necessary, to keep a uniform shape.

Hydrangeas. Prune after blooming period, removing old branches that have a tendency to rest on the ground. Remove all stems that have flowered and keep the strong new shoots that haven't bloomed. Cut one-half inch above a healthy pair of buds.

Spring-flowering trees and shrubs. Prune after the blooming period. Keep dead wood removed at all times. Oleander, viburnum, cassia, and ligustrum require thinning and heading back to maintain desired form. Cut all branches of spirea back halfway to encourage branching and thus more flowers.

Golden rain trees. These respond well to pruning because they grow rapidly, but they should be shaped while young. Keep dead wood removed.

Crape myrtle. If full clusters of bloom are desired, crape myrtles should be pruned after old blooms fade in the fall. Flowers appear on new growth in the spring. Keep suckers and weak, spindly branches removed.

India hawthorn (*Rhaphiolepis* spp.). This slow-growing shrub requires very little pruning. Some varieties have several blooming cycles. Prune after each blooming period. Pinching the tips of limbs two or three times a year will encourage branching and produce dense growth. Runaway branches should be removed at their source. Remove suckers that seem to come from root stock.

Firethorn (*Pyracantha coccinea*). This bushy, sprawling, fast-growing shrub requires pruning for control. Prune to create a specimen bush, tree, hedge, or vine or to keep it espaliered on a wall or loosely wound around a post or banister. Berries form on new growth. For more berries, remove all old berry-producing branches as soon as berries have dropped. When branches are headed back, the new growth comes out in bunches, thus producing more flowers and berries. If you do major pruning on a large plant just after berries fall in late spring, you should prune with caution because these plants have wicked thorns.

Wisteria vines. These vines are vigorous growers that need to be trimmed extensively to stimulate spring bloom and control growth. Prune heavily after flowering and again in November or December. Trim new shoots back to within six buds from the base of the branch and cut out all weak wood. Fall pruning should not be as severe as the spring-summer postbloom pruning. Root pruning around one side of the vine in December sometimes encourages blooms.

Camellias, gardenias, and azaleas. These flowering shrubs require very little pruning. Generally, freeze damage is confined to leaf and flower bud burn. Damaged buds will usually drop, which means a loss of spring blossoms. Prune any dead stems after the usual flowering period is over.

Azaleas don't respond well to drastic pruning. Prune a little here and there each year to maintain shape.

Fruit trees. These trees should be pruned during their dormant period, in the winter months after a cold snap. They include pears, peaches, apples, persimmons, plums, and grapevines.

Citrus trees. Pruning requires an educated guess. The best time is to catch them between the fruit crop and the blossoms. This time period varies in central and southern Florida due to the variety of fruit and variance in climate, but it should be about February. However, if the weather warms up suddenly, blossoms can seem to appear overnight. Diseased and dead wood can be cut out anytime.

Suckers should be removed as soon as they appear. Suckers are water sprouts that spring up from the base of a grafted tree. They grow rapidly in an upright position and are easily identified by their large, sharp thorns. These vigorous sprouts absorb nutrients needed by the bearing limbs of the tree.

Hanging branches and branches that extend beyond the canopy should be removed in order to maintain a pleasing shape. Cut well back at the junction of a large limb because snipping ends of limbs on the outside of trees produces excess foliage with weak stems. Branches have to be strong enough to accommodate the weight of mature fruit.

To allow light and air circulation, the inside of fruit trees should not be crowded. Excess foliage, small sprouts, and limbs should be removed from the interior. When two limbs cross and rub together, remove one of them.

In case of a severe freeze, don't prune citrus trees until late spring after new growth appears. Citrus can be killed down below the graft. When this happens it is best to start over with a new tree because root stock growth may or may not bear fruit; if it does, the fruit will be inferior.

Tropical and subtropical species. Pruning of plants that fall into this category is generally determined by the amount of freeze damage they sustain. (See the section on postfreeze plant care.) Otherwise, pruning simply means keeping the plants well groomed.

The tops of tropical and semitropical species that make an unsightly, mushy mess after being frozen can be removed immediately without damage to their root systems. These plants include banana, canna, bird-of-paradise (*Strelitzia* spp.), arrowhead plant (*Syngonium* spp.), and lilies. They will usually sprout new shoots in the spring. However, shock from a freeze will most likely upset the normal blooming cycle.

Palm trees. Pruning palms simply means trimming off leaves as they turn brown and become unsightly. The part of the stem that is left attached to the tree when the leaves are cut is called a boot. Boots can be left on or removed to give the trunk a smooth appearance. Floral branches should be removed before they dry out and litter the ground below. Severe pruning of outer leaves is necessary when palms are transplanted. However, palms make their growth from center leaves, and these should not be disturbed.

Summarizing Pruning

- Learn how to prune and do it right.
- Use proper tools and keep them sharp.
- Know your plants (growth habits; size and shape when mature; soil, fertilizer, water, and light requirements; common enemies; diseases; and seasonal color).
- Understand the purpose for pruning each plant and the best time of year to do it. Be conscious of what you wish to accomplish.

- Clean cutting blades well with alcohol or a bleach solution after pruning diseased wood to avoid spreading disease and fungus.

- Keep dead, broken, and diseased wood removed.

- When two limbs cross and rub together, remove one.

- Remove some of the limbs that grow inward when necessary to let air and sunshine inside.

- Keep in mind that pruning stimulates new growth.

- Guide, rather than force, the shape you desire.

- Cut just above a bud, and don't leave stubs even when pruning small shoots and twigs. Leafless stubs seldom grow new foliage. They decay and allow fungus and disease to develop.

- Avoid excessive pruning at any one time because the shock may be too great. Take your time and do it right.

- Grow new plants from your cuttings.

WIND, SALT, COLD, AND DROUGHT

Seacoast gardening is beset with a number of special problems such as constant wind, abrasion from blowing sand, and exposure to salt spray. In addition to soils that are infertile, a combination of salt in the air and salt in well water means a hostile environment for many growing things. The presence of chlorides (salts) in the water is a serious problem.

Florida weather conditions that are extreme and unpredictable add to the woes of gardeners. We can have a bitter freeze as early as December and as late as mid-March, or we can have a delightful winter without any severely cold weather. We rarely experience more than two nights in one winter when the temperature falls below freezing.

For a list of our most cold-hardy plants, consult the calendars for the winter months (chapter 5). A few suggestions also appear later in this chapter and in table 1.

Salt burn is a particular problem close to the sea. It is manifested by brown tips on leaves, which gradually involve the whole leaf and eventually cause the plant to die. High salt levels in the soil dehydrate and burn the roots, thereby reducing water uptake. Salt spray from the ocean can coat the foliage to the extent that it interferes with photosynthesis. Types of plants vary in their ability to tolerate salt. The roots of some plants will tolerate more salt than the foliage.

There are several ways in which dooryard gardeners can partially overcome the problems caused by wind, salt, cold, and drought.

Soil preparation. Proper soil preparation is the place to start. Incorporate as much organic material into the soil as possible, including compost, peat, black dirt, and animal manures. Soil building in Florida is an ongoing, never-ending gardening procedure because much of the soil in the state is porous sand.

Mulching. Use a good mulch to help retain moisture, to discourage weeds that rob nutrients and water, and to keep the hot sun from drying the topsoil. Good mulches include partially decomposed compost, oak leaves, hay, pine straw, shredded cypress, and pine bark. Stones and plastic sheeting can be used as mulch but are not as satisfactory as organic mulches. Plastic sheeting should have a layer of organic mulch over the top to deflect heat.

Fertilizing. Use organic (commercial or seasoned animal manure) and acid-forming fertilizers in sandy alkaline soils. Apply light applications more often rather than heavy applications less often because they leach out rapidly. Always wet the ground before applying fertilizer and then water well. Keep fertilizer away from stems and foliage. It is frequently necessary to supplement fertilizer with minor elements. (See the section on fertilizer in chapter 1.)

Watering. Use good management practices in applying water. If salts are high in your well water, follow well irrigations with a thorough soaking with city water. Flood the ground and rinse the foliage.

Planning. When planning your landscape, choose plants that are wind-, salt-, cold-, and drought-tolerant as much as possible, and by all means try to buy healthy plants. If your salt problem is severe, limit the number of plants needed for satisfactory landscaping and supplement the scene with groundcovers, decks, terrace tiles, bricks, gravel, or cement areas. A large wooden rain barrel can add to the decor while serving as a source of fresh water to use on plants.

Positioning plants. Where you place your plants is of utmost importance. Use walls, screens, dunes, fences, trees, and shrubbery as windbreaks to reduce wind, salt spray, and sand damage. Grouping plants that have the same general needs makes maintenance easier and creates less exposure.

Salt Tolerance

The salt tolerance of ornamentals in coastal locations places plants into two main categories: salt-tolerant and moderately salt-tolerant. The difference in exposures is the key to what you should plant where. Because they receive less exposure, many plants grow on gulf coast beaches that can't survive along the wide-open Atlantic coast. Zone 1, nearest the ocean, is considered an exposed environment. Only very hardy plants that are resistant to salt drift from the ocean and drought conditions will grow here. Zone 2, behind the first dune line, supports moderately salt-tolerant plants. These will tolerate salt spray but grow best when protected by fences, buildings, or plantings of salt-tolerant species.

Xeriscape

Perhaps the most important seacoast problem is the lack of fresh water. A landscaping technique known as xeriscape conserves water by the creative use of hardy, drought-tolerant plants.

There are a number of ecological advantages in developing a xeriscape plan. In addition to conservation of water, heightened aesthetic value results from using plants native to the area, and increased food is provided for native birds and animals. Saving water also results in lower maintenance in general.

The primary fundamentals of xeriscape gardening are planning and design, efficient irrigation, use of mulch, soil improvement, limited turf areas, plant selection, and appropriate maintenance—especially choosing plants that have a lower demand for water.

It is up to us, the thinking public, to abide conscientiously by water restrictions, which are necessary if we are to protect our future. Experienced seacoast gardeners will realize that we have been coping with many xeriscape fundamentals all along.

Choosing Plants

There are a number of plants that are salt- and wind-resistant but are not cold-hardy. The following list evaluates a number of plants for wind, salt, and drought.

Lawn grasses. In zone 1, St. Augustine (*Stenotaphrum secundatum*) or Bermuda (*Cynadon dactylon*) are the best choices. The Bahias will tolerate salt in the air but not in water.

Groundcovers. In zone 1, choose Algerian ivy (*Hedera canariensis*), coontie (*Zamia floridana*), English ivy (*Hedera helix*), euonymus (*E. fortunei*), fig marigold (*Glottiphyllum depressum*), ice plant (Hottentot fig), lantana (*L. montevidenesis* and *L. aculeata*), morning glory (*Ipomoea pes-caprae*), natal plum (dwarf, *Carissa* spp.), periwinkle (*Vinca* spp.), purslane (*Portulaca oleracea*), sea marigold (*Borrichia* spp.), seaside sunflower (*Helianthus debilis*), sea purslane (*Sesuvium portulcastrum*), sedum (*S. acre*), shore juniper (*Juni-perus conferta*), snake plant (*Sansevieria* spp.), and verbena (*Lantana depressa*).

In zone 2, choose asparagus fern (*Asparagus* spp.), dichondra (*D. caro-linensis*), dwarf lily turf (*Ophiopogon japonicum*, mondo grass), English ivy (*Hedera helix*), lily turf (*Liriope muscari* and *L. spicata*), oyster plant (*Rhoeo discolor*), purple queen (*Setcreasea* spp.), shore juniper (*Juniperus conferta*), verbena (*V.* spp.), wandering Jew (*Zebrina pendula*), and wedelia (*W. trilobata*).

Vines. In zone 1, choose Algerian ivy (*Hedera canariensis*), beach morning glory (*Ipomoea pes-caprae*), Confederate jasmine (*Trachelospermum jasmi-noides*), night-blooming cereus (*Hylocereus undatus*), and Virginia creeper (*Parthenocissus quinquefolia*).

In zone 2, choose allamanda (*A. cathartica*), bougainvillea (*B.* spp.), cape honeysuckle (*Tecomaria capensis*), coral (*Antigonon leptopus*), creeping fig (*Ficus pumila*), flame (*Pyrostegia ignea*), pink allamanda (*Mandevilla splendens*), wax plant (*Hoya carnosa*), and wandering Jew (*Zebrina pendula*).

Ornamental grasses. In zone 1, choose beach panic grass (*Panicum amarulum*), broom sedge (*Andropogon scoparius*), dwarf bamboo (*Bambusa multiplex*), giant reed (*Arundo donax*), and sea oats (*Uniola paniculata*).

In zone 2, choose umbrella plant (*Cyperus alternifolius*) and papyrus (*Cyperus papyrus*). Both are for water gardens but tolerate salt drift.

Annuals. In zone 1, choose African daisy, candytuft, dusty miller, periwinkle, sea marigold, and statice.

In zone 2, choose bachelor's button, bush daisy, calendula, coreopsis, cornflower, dianthus, gazania daisy, geranium, impatiens, petunia, phlox, salvia, snapdragon, sweet alyssum, pansy, and zinnia.

Perennials. In zone 1, choose bear grass (*Yucca smalliana*), coreopsis, dusty miller, gaillardia, goldenrod, periwinkle, and seaside sunflower.

In zone 2, choose black-eyed Susan (*Rudbeckia* spp.), butterfly weed, crinum lily, day lily (*Hemerocallis* spp.) gazania daisy, hollyhock, ixora, kalanchoe, moss rose, portulaca, Shasta daisy, salvia, sunflower, and verbena.

Flowering shrubs and trees. In zone 1, choose ardisia (*A. paniculata*), butterfly bush (*Buddleia* spp.), boxthorn (*Severinia buxifolia*), century plant (*Agave* spp.), crown-of-thorns (*Euphorbia milii*), India hawthorn (*Rhaphiolepis indica*), natal plum (*Carissa* spp.), prickly pear cactus (*Opuntia* spp.), thistle (*Echinop* spp.), yaupon holly (*Ilex vomitoria*), Adam's needle (*Yucca smalliana*), and Spanish bayonet (*Yucca aloifolia*).

In zone 2, choose acacia (*A. farnesiana*), bottle brush (*Callistemon rigidus*), holly (Burford, dahoon, East Palatka, yaupon, and Savannah), bird-of-paradise (*Strelitzia reginae* and *S. nicoli*), heather (*Cupheo hyssopifolia*), ixora (*I.* spp.), kalanchoe (*K.* spp.), mimosa (*Albizia julibrissin*), oleander (*Nerium oleander*), plumbago (*P. capensis*), rice-paper plant (*Tetrapanax papyriferus*), rose mallow (*Hibiscus moscheutos*), roses (*Rosa* spp.), and Texas sage (*Leucophyllum texanum*).

Evergreen shrubs. In zone 1, choose Adam's needle (*Yucca smalliana*, bear grass), boxthorn (*Severinia buxifolia*), century plant (*Agave* spp.), coontie (*Zamia floridana*), euonymus (*E.* spp.), fatsia (*F. japonica*), firethorn (*Pyracantha coccinea*), India hawthorn (*Rhaphiolepis indica*), juniper (*Juniperus* spp.), ligustrum (*L. lucidum* and *L. japonicum*), natal plum (*Carissa grandiflora*), pittosporum (*P. tobira*), plumbago (*P. capensis*), podocarpus (*P.* spp.), prickly pear (*Opuntia* spp.), rice-paper plant (*Tetrapanax papyriferus*), sea grape (*Coccoloba uvifera* and *C.*

grandifolia), silverthorn (*Elaeagnus pungens*), Spanish bayonet (*Yucca aloifolia*), and wax myrtle (*Myrica cerifera*).

In zone 2, choose arborvitae (*Thuja orientalis*), euonymus (*E. fortunei*), Feijoa guava (*F. sellowiana*), ligustrum (*L. japonicum*, wax privet), nandina (*N. domestica*), oleander (*Nerium oleander*), podocarpus (*P. macrophylla*), and viburnum (*V. odoratissimum* and *V. suspensum*).

Trees. In zone 1, choose Australian pine (*Casuarina equisetifolia*), magnolia (*M. grandiflora*), scrub oak (*Quercus* spp.), prickly ash (*Zanthoxylum americanum*, toothache tree), red bay (*Persea boronia*), and wax myrtle (*Myrica cerifera*).

In zone 2, choose bottle brush (*Callistemon rigidus*), golden rain (*Koelreuteria elegans*), Jerusalem thorn (*Parkinsonia aculeata*), loquat (*Eriobotrya japonica*), mimosa tree (*Albizia julibrissin*), Norfolk Island pine (*Araucaria excelsa*), loblolly bay (*Gordonia lasianthus*), red cedar (*Juniperus silicicola*), and sycamore (*Platanus occidentalis*, buttonwood, plane tree). Among pines (*Pinus* spp.), choose longleaf (*P. palustris*), sand or scrub (*P. clausa*), and slash (*P. elliotti*).

Palms (northern Florida). In zone 1, choose cabbage (*Sabal palmetto*), coontie (*Zamia* spp.), and saw palmetto (*Serenoa repens*).

In zone 2, choose European fan (*Chamaerops humilis*), pindo (*Butia capitata* or *Cocos australis*, jelly palm), Phoenix date (*P. canariensis*, Canary Island, pineapple), and sago (*Cycas revoluta*).

Palms (central Florida). In zone 1, choose cabbage (*Sabal palmetto*), blue palmetto (*Sabal minor*), saw palmetto (*Serenoa repens*), and scrub palmetto (*Sabal etonia*).

In zone 2, choose lady (*Raphis* spp.), pindo (*Butia capitata* or *Cocos australis*, jelly palm), Chinese fan (*Livistona chinensis*), European fan (*Chamaerops humilis*), fishtail (*Caryota ureus*), petticoat (*Washingtonia robusta*), queen (*Cocos plumosa* or *Arecastrum romanzoffianum*), sago (*Cycas circinalis* and *C. revoluta*), saw cabbage (*Paurotis wrightii*), and windmill (*Trachycarpus fortunei*). Phoenix date species include Canary Island date or pineapple (*P. canariensis*), Senegal date (*P. reclinata*), pygmy date (*P. roebeleni*), and cliff date (*P. rupicola*). Pygmy and cliff are dwarf and require protection from frost.

Palms (southern Florida). All of the previously listed palms will thrive in southern Florida. Other interesting palms include coconut

(*Cocos nucifera*), silver (*Coccothrinax argentata*), solitaire (*Seforthia elegans*), royal (*Roystonea regia, R. elata,* and *R. oleracea*), thatch (*Thrinax parviflora*), Manila (*Veitchia merrillii*), and yellow butterfly (*Chrysalidocarpus lutescens*).

❀

Here is a list of salt-tolerant plants resistant to cold below thirty-two degrees.

Trees. These include apple, arborvitae, bay (sweet, loblolly), buckeye, camphor, cedar, cherry laurel, crape myrtle, cypress, dogwood, hickory, American holly (Burford, dahoon, East Palatka, Savannah, and yaupon), India hawthorn, Jerusalem thorn, loquat, magnolia, maple, mimosa, mulberry, oak (laurel, live, and water), peach, persimmon, pine (Australian, sand, slash, and long leaf), prickly ash, redbud, sweet gum, sycamore, and wax myrtle.

Shrubs. These include bamboo, boxthorn, cactus (prickly pear), century plant, euonymus, fatsia, holly, India hawthorn, juniper, ligustrum, pittosporum, podocarpus, pyracantha, silverthorn, viburnum, and wax myrtle.

❀

The following salt-tolerant plants will freeze down but will usually come back from their roots.

Groundcovers. These include asparagus fern, dichondra, lantana, wedelia, natal plum, oyster plant, periwinkle, snake plant, and verbena.

Vines. These include allamanda, beach morning glory, bougainvillea, coral vine, and night-blooming cereus.

Grasses. These include pampas, sea oats, and umbrella.

Annuals. Black-eyed Susan, periwinkle, phlox, and impatiens all reseed themselves.

Shrubs. These include acacia, aloe, carissa, oleander, bird-of-paradise, podocarpus, rice-paper plant, sea grape, and well-established hibiscus.

POSTFREEZE SUGGESTIONS

Winter months in the southeastern part of the United States are generally unpredictable. We can have temperate years, very cold years with a number of hard freezes, or anything in between. Gardeners in Florida learn that there are two factors in managing freeze damage—preparation and management.

Preparation

Because of an abundance of coastline, nearness to the Gulf Stream, and many rivers and lakes, Florida benefits from warmth coming off the water. Nevertheless, from December through March, temperatures can drop to frost or freezing overnight. These interruptions of our moderate climate make it wise to choose as many hardy plants as we can for basic landscaping. We can enjoy delicate plants but must also be prepared to protect those we can and gracefully accept the loss of others. Many of the tropicals are relatively inexpensive and can be replaced with ease in the spring.

Management of Freeze Damage

When a freeze is preceded by a few weeks of cool weather, plants have a better chance of making a comeback than when the fall weather remains quite warm before the temperature suddenly drops below thirty-two degrees. Some plants have a natural protective device that, with the advent of low temperatures, enables them to survive. Cool weather brings on dormancy. This means that most of the sap descends to the root system so that the sap doesn't freeze within the plant, swell, and rupture cells. Ruptured cells are no longer able to transmit water and nutrients.

Plants that are hardy—India hawthorn, ligustrum, viburnum, holly, juniper, cedar, magnolia, cherry laurel, crape myrtle, loquat, euonymus, silverthorn (*Elaeagnus* spp.), podocarpus, nandina—welcome cold weather because it gives them a dormant, or inactive, period in which to prepare for spring growth and flowering.

Another point that favors plants' survival after a freeze is a slow thaw-out period that allows time for them to adapt. It's important that they are watered properly following a freeze. Water well when a freeze is forecast and again as soon as possible afterward. Wind and cold have a tendency to dehydrate foliage, meaning that additional water needs to be supplied. Generally, it is desirable to turn off sprinklers before a freeze.

If you have covered some plants, and if temperatures remain quite low following a freeze, it is all right to leave covering on throughout the days. However, if the sun comes out and temperatures rise, you should uncover your plants and water them well. Warm sunshine can turn the moist air under the coverings into steam, and plants that were not seriously damaged by the cold can be injured by heat.

The only way we can determine the true extent of damage after a freeze is to wait and see. Some plants that seem to have escaped can continue to die gradually for years.

Your cleanup program can start as soon as you can tell which plants need help. Obviously, soft, slimy foliage and stems; frozen flower buds; small, dead branches; brown leaves; and any plants you don't really care about can be removed as soon as they exhibit these conditions. But don't do any major pruning of hardwoods until spring.

Citrus trees. Damage to citrus trees is obvious after a hard freeze, but the extent of damage can't be determined for several weeks or months. If the temperature drops low enough for the sap in the trunk and limbs to freeze, the bark will split and crack in a few months.

Bananas. Frozen banana leaves can be removed immediately. New leaves will appear from the stalk in late spring unless the stalk was frozen. If it is frozen, it will begin to get soft in a week or two. When this happens, cut the stalk off at the ground level. New plants will generally come up from the roots in the spring.

Birds-of-paradise. Leaf stalks will turn brown and collapse soon after freezing. You may remove them or leave them to cover the plant to give some protection in the event of another freeze. Don't wait any later than March to prune leaves. It will take twelve to fifteen months before you can expect flowers again.

Roses. If your roses were in good condition and you mulched them well, they should have undergone little damage. February is the time to prune them. Keep up a monthly fertilizer program and spray as indicated. Keep them watered.

Azaleas and camellias. Damage to azaleas and camellias is usually limited to flower buds and stems. Badly damaged buds will drop, but slightly damaged buds might show brown tips or spots on flowers when the buds open. The leaves of azaleas can look black and terrible following a freeze and still bring forth new foliage in the spring along with the blossoms. A nutritional spray can help them over this setback.

Gardenias. When gardenias show marked leaf damage, they will usually recover with proper fertilizer and water. They will probably need to be sprayed with a pesticide because mealybugs and scales often attack plants that are in a weakened condition. Unlike azaleas, gardenias are very slow to recover and are prone to show cracking of the bark months after being exposed to freezing weather.

Hardwoods. After the last average freeze-warning date (mid-March), prune your hardwoods. Start on the outer tips of the branches, moving inward until you reach healthy, live wood. Remember that pruning stimulates growth: If you prune too soon, new leaves will sprout and may be killed in another freeze. Most plants can't survive two freezes in one winter.

Plants that can be cut down. The entire tops of some plants—rubber, philodendron, Japanese rice paper, ginger, schefflera, ferns, some bromeliads, ixora, croton, and poinsettia—may be killed. However, sometimes the roots are able to send up new shoots when the weather warms up in the spring. These plants should be pruned to the ground in early spring, watered, fertilized, and given time to produce new growth before you declare them dead.

Summarizing Postfreeze Care

Protect plants as much as possible during times of freezing temperatures. Some ways to do this are to cover with corrugated boxes, blankets, sheets, mattress covers, or drop cloths; mulch heavily; sand-bank trunks; and wrap banana and papaya trunks in newspapers. A tent held up by poles can be built over larger plants and a sixty- to seventy-five-watt light bulb placed inside. The hot bulb should not rest on limbs or touch foliage. If plastic is used for the tent, it should not touch foliage.

- Water well before and after a freeze.

- Clean and tidy up, but prune only soft and decaying foliage after a freeze.

- Wait until after danger of last predicted frost (usually March) to do heavy pruning.

- When spring comes, replant where necessary and use plants that are cold-tolerant. Reevaluate your landscape and redesign.

- When buying new plants, choose cold-hardy ones.

CHAPTER 3

❀

Specific Plants

ROSES

According to fossil study, roses have been native American wildflowers for more than 30 million years, but it wasn't until September 1986 that the rose was designated our national flower. Long known as the "queen of flowers," the rose has been a favorite of the American people. It symbolizes love, friendship, peace, and devotion. Roses are grown in every state and enjoy wide popularity.

There are about one thousand varieties of roses, each responding differently to various climates and soils. Different types have been bred for different purposes: hybrid teas on a single long stem for cut flowers; floribundas, which flower in clusters, usually low to the ground, making them perfect for borders or mass beds; grandifloras, which have multiple blooms on one stem and are tall growers good for background plantings or accents; compact miniatures, with small plants and flowers for containers or patios; and climbers.

Growing roses in warm seacoast areas requires a little extra knowledge but can be done successfully. The rewards are great. It doesn't matter if you have one bush or a hundred: Each new bud is a source of inspiration. Start with a few plants and increase the number as you gain experience. Just remember that roses require constant attention.

Planting Roses

When to plant. February, March, and April are my favorite months to plant roses. Container-grown bushes can be planted in almost any month of the year except for the very hot ones, but bare-root stock should be planted in cool weather.

Selection. The first step in planting roses is to select healthy vigorous plants grown to thrive in a warm climate. Roses planted on grafted *Rosa fortuniana* rootstock are the best choice for central and southern Florida soil, but *Dr. Huey* rootstock is also used.

There are many types of roses but only four basic classifications: hybrid teas (one-to-a-stem flowers that are perfect for cutting), floribundas (bloom in clusters), grandifloras (featuring multiple blooms on one stem long enough for cutting), and miniatures (diminutive forms of hybrid teas and floribundas).

Suggestions for roses that met warm climate standards include three climbers: Lady Banks' (*Rosa banksiae*, white or yellow cluster blossoms), Seven Sisters (pink cluster blossoms), and Don Juan (double, deep red blossoms on long canes with a heavy fragrance).

Louis Philipe (red), Bonica (pink), and Carefree Wonder (pink), are vigorous, ever-blooming cluster roses that require minimum care. They are particularly impressive when grouped in beds or mass plantings or grown as a low broad hedge.

Two old favorites with the ability to flourish in all regions are Mister Lincoln (a dark red hybrid tea with an exciting fragrance) and Tropicana (a coral orange grandiflora with a fruity fragrance and long-lasting blossoms).

Fragrant beauties include Perfume Delight (a deep pink hybrid tea with large, satiny flowers and a rich, spicy perfume), Brandy (a large golden apricot hybrid tea with a delightful fragrance), and Broadway (a hybrid tea with buds that open yellow but each day the petals combine traces of pink that intensify into rose by the end of the week. It stays in bloom from spring to frost, has a pleasant fragrance, and will last for a week as a cut flower).

Queen Elizabeth is known as the rose of choice for a one-rose garden. A grandiflora, it is one of the most highly rated roses for vigor and disease resistance. It is radiant pink and is available as a climber or a tree rose.

Peace, the world's most famous rose, is a hybrid tea with large blossoms that have a slight fragrance. Its petals are pale yellow fringed in pink.

Where to plant. Choosing the proper planting site is critical because roses need at least six hours of sun a day. Morning sun is preferred over hot afternoon sun, which can bleach flowers and burn leaves. Also, morning sun hastens the evaporation of dew, thus reducing the potential for fungus infection.

Soil preparation. Roses do best in slightly acidic (pH 6.5), loamy soil with a high humus content. Therefore, sandy soil has to be amended to increase moisture retention and to supply necessary nutrients. It is a good idea to have your soil tested to determine the pH and the presence, or absence, of necessary nutrients.

Here is a general formula recommended for rose soil mixture in an area where the soil is sandy and alkaline. Retain half of the sandy soil dug from the planting hole and shovel it into a wheelbarrow. With it mix in three to four gallons of black compost or peat; one to two gallons of dry, aged manure; and one cup of fertilizer suitable for roses (8-4-7). One cup of superphosphate and one cup of magnesium sulphate may be added for an extra boost. If your soil is alkaline, add one-half cup of wettable sulphur. If your soil tests too acidic, omit the sulphur and add one cup of dolomite.

How to plant. Rose plants need to be spaced three to six feet apart, depending on the type and its growth pattern. When buying your plants, try to learn as much as you can about the growing habits and mature size of each bush.

When planting a container-grown rose, dig a hole twice as large as the root ball of the plant. Place several inches of partially decomposed compost in the bottom of the hole to help retard drainage until the plant has had time to become established. Plant the rose on a slight mound, at the depth it was in the purchased container. The bud union should stand at least two to three inches above the mound. (The bud union is the bulge where the stem joins the rootstock.) Leave the soil slightly ditched around the plant to hold water and mulch.

Planting bare-root roses requires a bit more skill. When buying plants, carefully examine the canes and roots. There should be several sturdy, well-branched roots. Roots and canes should not appear dry and shriveled or show any signs of disease. Plants must be kept cool and moist until you are able to plant them. Before planting, trim away any broken roots and then soak roots in water for a few hours or overnight. Dig a hole large enough to accommodate the root system without crowding. Build a soil cone six to eight inches high in the bottom of the hole. Rest the plant on top of the cone, spreading the roots out, down, and around the sides of the cone.

As you fill the hole with your special soil mix, adjust the plant so that the bud union is slightly above the soil line. Fill the hole about two-thirds full of soil mix, and water well. Let water soak in completely. Then fill the rest of the hole with soil, firming it gently by hand (not foot) as you fill. Continue to soak with water by pushing the end of the hose down and around the roots to finish settling the soil. Keep the soil moist, not wet, until the plant shows its first flush of leaves.

Tending Roses

Mulch. Roses need to be mulched with about three inches of pine needles, shredded cypress bark, partly decomposed compost, or hay to help hold moisture and discourage weeds. Rosebush roots grow in a shallow, spreading pattern; so when adding new mulch as needed, take care not to disturb the root system. If there's any sign of insect invasion, dust an insecticide around the bush before applying new mulch. Keep the mulch at the base of each plant clean because fallen leaves infected with black spot encourage spread of the disease. In order to prevent stem rot and insect invasion, don't pile the mulch against the trunks.

Fertilizer. Wait until it is apparent that the new bush is thriving and putting out new growth before starting to use a commercial fertilizer.

Roses are heavy feeders. New plants usually need about one-half cup of fertilizer each month. Older bushes require more, depending upon their size and age. A general, balanced fertilizer such as 6-6-6 or 8-8-8 (with minor elements) should suffice. A fertilizer especially balanced for roses—8-4-7—is available. It is a good idea to supplement about twice each year with seasoned dairy manure. For fast results, a foliar fertilizer can be mixed with water and sprayed on the leaves. There is also a systemic rose and flower fertilizer that feeds and protects against insects such as aphids, leafhoppers, and spider mites.

Control of disease and pests. A regular spray program is necessary in hot, humid climates to control fungal diseases such as black spot and powdery mildew as well as insects. Products are available that contain both an insecticide and a fungicide. Signs of insects are easy to see because they chew leaves and petals, curl leaves, make webs, and deform buds. Nematodes that attack the root systems are a problem in some localities, but *Rosa fortuniana* rootstock is resistant.

Black spot is the biggest problem with which we have to cope. In addition to a regular spray program, you should keep all affected leaves picked off the plants and picked up from the ground.

Watering. Roses need to be watered several times weekly. It is best to water with a hose or a soaker to avoid wetting the foliage. Choose a sunny planting site that is out of the reach of sprinklers and shielded from the wind.

Protection. Temperature changes affect the growth and overall health of roses. The buds react to cold weather by curling up to retain warmth and failing to open normally. Damaged buds should be cut off to stimulate development of new buds. Roses can tolerate low temperatures down to fifteen degrees; however, they need some protection when there is a sudden extreme change in the weather. In case of a freeze warning, mound the base of the plant with soil or compost. If the plant is not too large, cover with a corrugated box.

Pruning. Pruning roses correctly is of the utmost importance, as is knowing the right way to remove the blooms for cut flowers. The general rule in the warmer coastal areas allows for fairly severe pruning in February to remove weak stems and control the size of the plant. Light pruning can be done in October simply to groom the plants. Keep dead wood removed and spent roses cut from your plants at all times. When cutting a bloom, go down no further than the first five-leaflet leaf on the outer side of a stem. If you are going to grow roses, attend one of the clinics held each year by your county extension service and learn the right way to prune.

BULBS IN GENERAL

"Consider the lilies—how they grow." They grow from bulbs.

Plants loosely spoken of as bulbs or lilies actually fall into one of five forms of thickened underground roots, stems, and leaves adapted to food storage and reproduction. These categories are true bulbs, rhizomes, corms, tubers, and tuberous roots. Although different, all share one characteristic that sets them apart from other plants—their marvelous natural storehouse of plant food.

It is said that bulbs are plants for all seasons and no garden is complete without them. Generally, they require less care but produce more beauty and pleasure than most other plants.

Types of Bulbs

Of the several different types of underground roots, some are referred to as lilies even though they are not true bulbs. Although it isn't important for the average gardener to know the differences, here are the definitions of these various roots.

True bulbs. True bulbs are a complete, dormant embryo of a future plant. The fleshy structure is covered by scales or layers of tissue (leaf bases modified for storage) that store the plant's food for growth. The bud of a true bulb is at the top in the center. Examples are tulip, amaryllis, crinum, and narcissus.

Rhizomes. These underground stems spread by creeping, producing shoots above and roots below. Plants with rhizomes include calla, canna, most grasses, bearded iris, day lily, and liriope.

Corms. Corms consist of a solid mass of storage tissue that is actually a storage stem. They have buds (eyes) just like bulbs. Gladiolus is an example.

Tubers. Tubers are composed of a solid mass of storage tissue with eyes on top. They include caladium and gloriosa lily.

Tuberous roots. Tuberous roots have food-storing roots. However, the bud eyes are not on the roots but on the base of the plant's stem. They bear no buds or eyes such as rhizomes have. Examples include coontie, some begonias, and oxalis.

Propagation and Care of Plants Grown from Bulbs

Bulbs are able to provide nourishment for themselves in the most diverse kinds of soil and conditions. Even after lying dormant for months and enduring drought, frost, or searing heat, they can spring back to life and continue their species when conditions improve. However, they will not flower again unless their leaves have time to replenish the bulbs' depleted food supply for the coming year. For this reason the foliage must not be cut until the leaves begin to turn yellow.

Soil preparation. As with other plants that bloom, soil preparation is important for bulbs. Before planting, turn sandy soil to a depth of eight to ten inches and mix in lots of organic matter such as decomposed compost, manures, and peat (black dirt). Bulbs need a good source of balanced nutrients in order to build a healthy root system. You can help by adding about two teaspoons of a bed mix fertilizer under each bulb at planting time. (Bed mix is a blend of all-natural organic nitrogen with phosphate, potash, and certain essential minor elements. It will not burn roots.)

Planting. The only real difference in the way in which various bulbs are planted is the depth of planting and the spacing between the bulbs. There should be loose soil beneath the bulb to encourage root growth. Place the bulb in a hole with its pointed end, or buds, facing up. Fill the hole, firm the soil around the bulb, and water well. Fall and spring are considered the best seasons for bulb planting, but several kinds can be planted almost anytime. See the section on bulbs in particular later in this chapter.

Most bulbs do best in sun or high shade with moderate moisture, but a few prefer constant moisture, while others thrive in fairly dry conditions. It is best to plant on a slight rise or where good drainage is assured because too much water will cause some bulbs to rot. Most bulbs need to be dug and replanted after three to five years, when their clumps get too crowded.

Mulching. Mulching helps retain moisture and discourage weeds. Organic materials are best because they add nutrients to the soil. See the section on mulch in chapter 1.

Feeding. For fall and spring plantings, feeding is different. If you prepared your beds properly and are planting in the fall, very little extra fertilizer will be needed. A couple of applications of a general product (6-6-6) during the winter months should be sufficient. Spring plantings should be fertilized to promote blooms, using an application of bulb fertilizer (4-8-8; 4-11-11; or another low-nitrogen, high-phosphorus, high-potassium formula). Avoid overfertilizing and overwatering in the winter months.

Flowers. To prevent seed formation, remove blooms after they fade. This allows the strength to go to the foliage and thus to the bulb, providing vitality for next year's bloom. The foliage should not be cut until it has turned yellow. However, in the warmer climates, where the leaves stay green and continue to thrive, it is permissible to cut them off about six inches above the bulb several months after the bloom has faded. This slows down the growing process and gives the bulb a chance to store up nutrients for next year's blossoms.

Problems. Growing most bulbous plants presents few problems. Some bulbs have a tendency to sink deeper and deeper into the earth each year as their roots grow downward, which eventually causes them to stop blooming. To prevent or correct this, you need to dig and replant bulbs at the proper depth.

Caterpillars, grasshoppers, aphids, mealybugs, red spiders, and fungi have to be dealt with from time to time, but each type can be controlled by spraying with the proper pesticide.

Erratic winter weather confuses bulbs. If the winter is unusually warm, the spring bulbs may sprout too early. Although most bulbous plants are cold-hardy, new spring foliage can be damaged by a late freeze.

In subtropical areas, many nontropical bulbs will not flower unless they are given a cold period (that is, dug up and stored in the refrigerator). See the section on bulbs in particular later in this chapter.

Bulbs in Particular

On the whole, plants that grow from bulbs are easy to care for and offer a variety of blooms as diverse as their names. Listed here are the bulbs that are most commonly and successfully grown in the southeastern coastal areas. To plant them, prepare the soil as recommended in the section on bulbs in general, unless otherwise indicated.

Bulbs that are salt-tolerant and do well near the ocean include amaryllis, canna, crinum, rain, and day. Ginger, Easter, calla, gladiolus, caladium, blood, and gloriosa will burn and should be planted behind the second dune line and protected from salt spray.

In hot parts of Florida and around the gulf coast, many of the tropical bulbs discussed in this section can bloom throughout the year. In northern Florida, where the winters get much cooler and allow a longer dormant period, additional bulbs can be grown for spring or summer—daffodil, allium, fritillaria, hyacinth, jonquil, and tulip.

Specific Bulbs

Lily-of-the-Nile, African lily (*Agapanthus africanus*). Rhizomes of these lilies are best planted in fall or winter. They will then send up thick, fleshy strap leaves in the spring. Clusters of blue or white flowers on leafless flower stalks will follow throughout the summer and fall. Plant agapanthus in sturdy containers or in the ground in light shade, twenty-four inches apart. Set them so that the tops of the roots are just below the surface of the soil. A rhizome is a creeping stem and should not be covered deeply. Unlike most bulb plants, agapanthus blooms best when its roots are crowded. Fertilize during the growing season, using a general product every couple of months. However, during the rest of the year withhold fertilizer and keep them on the dry side. Propagate by dividing roots in the fall.

Hurricane (*Amaryllis vittata* spp.). Varieties of amaryllis may be solid-colored or striped, and some are fragrant. They can be planted almost all year round and are easy to grow. Planting at several-week intervals from September to February will give a succession of bloom from spring well into summer. They have slender strap leaves, but the blooms appear on leafless stalks. Each stalk may bear three to six trumpet-shaped blossoms that can be three or four inches across. They usually start to bloom in April.

Plant amaryllis bulbs in containers or in the ground, in high shade or in morning sun. Space them at least six inches apart. Don't plant them too deep. One-third of the bulb should be in the soil and two-thirds above the soil, or they won't bloom well.

When bulbs are left in the ground, fertilize about three times a year. Use a bulb fertilizer (4-8-8) in the spring, a general fertilizer (6-6-6) after flowering and in October. Water sparingly until growth begins; then increase moisture and apply fertilizer. After the blooming period, decrease water gradually to increase dormancy. If your plants are in containers, permit a rest period by turning them on their sides in August with no water or fertilizer. Set pots upright and start watering again in the fall in order to repeat the cycle. Plants grown from imported bulbs take about three months from planting until blossoms. However, replanted bulbs in warm climates will generally not bloom until spring regardless of when you replant them.

You can propagate amaryllis from seeds gathered from mature pods or from new bulbs that form around the mother bulb. Amaryllis grown from seed won't bloom for several years.

After amaryllis bulbs bloom, they hurriedly store up next year's energy and then produce a cluster of baby bulbs. These babies continue to depend upon their mothers for nourishment. If they are not removed, the mother bulb will not have enough energy to bloom next spring. Also, the beds will become overcrowded, plants will take nourishment from each other, and there will be no blossoms.

Generally, bulbs should be dug about every three years in the fall to transplant. Cutting off all but about six inches of the foliage makes them easier to handle. The baby bulbs should be transplanted immediately to allow them to grow larger because they don't bloom their first year. The larger bulbs can be transplanted right away or stored in a dry place for a month or two of rest.

Caladium (C. spp.). Caladiums can be purchased as tubers, seedlings, or full-size plants during the spring and summer. They are not true bulbs but are thickened underground stems with many buds (eyes) present over their surfaces.

The tubers are planted in late March when the ground starts to warm up to add quick color to summer's landscape. If you wish to get a head start, plant some indoors in pots on a sunny windowsill. They can be used as container plants or transplanted into the yard (after danger of frost) to fill in spaces. Caladiums are grown for their decorative heart- or spear-shaped leaves, which come in a number of sizes. Most leaves have smooth edges, but some are ruffled. There is an endless combination of delicate to splashy colors available. To avoid damage to the leaves, protect the planting areas from sprinklers and wind.

Try caladiums in hanging baskets or window boxes, as a border for trees, along pathways and flower beds, or as mass color in a large bed.

These plants thrive in subdued light and are perfect for brightening a shady spot. Morning or filtered sunlight is best because full sun can fade the colors in the leaves.

When planting tubers outdoors, it's best to keep the buds facing up. Plant in furrows or individual holes nine to fifteen inches apart, depending upon the variety (leaf size and height). Place bed mix fertilizer in the hole, cover with about one inch of soil, firm the soil around the bulb, mulch, and water. The first leaves should be visible within three to six weeks, depending upon soil and weather conditions.

Four to six weeks after planting, apply a general fertilizer (6-6-6). Repeat once more about midsummer; then reduce fertilizer toward the end of summer. Because of evaporation from the large leaf surface, caladiums need to be kept uniformly moist.

Caladium tubers send up inconspicuous flowers on a leafless stalk. Remove flowers as soon as they appear to prolong the life of the plant. In the fall, when the foliage starts to turn yellow and flop over, carefully dig the tubers. Don't remove the leaves. When the soil that clings to the tubers has dried out, gently shake it off, place tubers in a box in a single layer, dust with fungicide/insecticide, and allow them to air dry for a few days. Then a gentle tug will remove the leaves. Store the tubers in an area where they won't freeze and that is well ventilated.

Do not refrigerate. In mild climates in well-drained soil, tubers may be left in the ground all year. However, you are taking a chance that some will rot or be eaten by squirrels.

The plants propagate from baby tubers, which you will find clinging to the mother bulb when you dig them in the fall. You can also propagate caladiums by cutting large tubers into pieces. When cutting tubers, leave at least two buds on each piece. Dust cut surfaces with a fungicide to prevent decay.

Calla lily (*Zantedeschia* spp.). Planting times for calla lily rhizomes range from September through January. Blooms can be expected throughout the spring months. Calla lilies are available in several sizes and colors, including white, pink, yellow, and gold. The ones with arrow-shaped leaves and large, white, spathe blossoms thrive in warm climates. They make impressive displays in planters or in beds. After the first bloom fades, cut the blossom stalk off to encourage more flowers.

Set rhizomes firmly about three inches beneath the surface and a foot apart. Full sun or light shade is preferred. The soil should be constantly moist but not wet. Feed monthly with a bulb fertilizer.

Calla lily foliage will turn yellow and die when the hot weather arrives. At that time the rhizomes can be dug or left in the ground. If the rhizomes are not dug, discontinue watering after the leaves turn yellow. Resume watering again in the fall to start growth.

Canna lily (*Canna generalis*). Requiring a minimum of care, canna lilies are especially good for background planting and mass color. Both the old garden delights and the newer hybrids with a variety of heights, bloom sizes, colors, and characteristics are available. Their erect leaves of green and bronze rise from underground rhizomes. Locate plants where they can show off colors but won't be too conspicuous when their foliage starts to turn brown.

March to early summer is the best time for planting. Place two teaspoons of bed mix fertilizer into the planting hole. Plant eighteen inches apart, three to four inches deep, in full sun. Be sure that the growing tips are on top and last year's roots on the bottom. Use a complete fertilizer and keep them well watered until they have a chance to develop roots. When the foliage is developing satisfactorily, apply a bulb fertilizer (4-8-8) once each month. Water copiously during growing time because they require much food and water for lush blossoms. A soaker hose is ideal. Water deeply once each week.

To encourage new bloom, snip off all faded blossoms and developing seed pods as they appear. Each stalk produces a panicle with many buds, with one or two flowers opening each day. A single stalk may bloom for two months.

When flowering stops and foliage begins to turn brown, the tops can be cut down to the ground. Canna roots can remain in the ground all winter; thus, they get a head start the following spring, when the rhizomes send up a number of new baby plants. Mulch the beds well, ease off on water, and stop the fertilizer until new shoots appear in the spring.

If it is necessary to dig the rhizomes, do so in late fall. Dust off the soil, sprinkle with fungicide/pesticide, and store in an airy box until March. Or they can be tied with a cord and hung during this rest period.

Cannas are relatively free from disease when they are grown in full sun, but watch out for caterpillars.

Crinum lily (*C.* spp.). Crinum lilies are salt-tolerant, so they make good seaside plants and are much to be desired in warm climates. They should be planted in the ground because they grow too fast and get too large to be considered for the average container. Bulbs can weigh up to twenty-five pounds and can have enormous mounds of strap-shaped leaves up to five feet tall. Clusters of fragrant flowers appear on leafless two- to three-foot stems. There are about one hundred species available in colors from white, pink, rosy red, and wine to striped.

Crinums prefer moist, well-drained soil in sun or shade. However, they seem to thrive in high shade. It is best to plant them in spring and fall and to space them at least two feet apart, depending upon the variety. Planting depth should be determined by the size of the bulb. Large bulbs may need to be as deep as six to eight inches in order to give the plant adequate support. Mulch well.

Most varieties can be left undisturbed indefinitely; but about every ten years, after the foliage has started to turn yellow, dig, thin, and transplant crowded old bulbs to new locations. Crinums flower most abundantly when the roots are crowded. Small bulbs that develop beside the larger ones can be removed at any time for propagation, but they won't bloom until they are about five years old.

Flowering time is generally in the spring and summer. During growth and flowering they should have plenty of water and an occasional light fertilization (6-6-6). Through the cool months they can be completely neglected. Crinums will tolerate poor soil, drought conditions, and neglect; they just won't flower as well.

Grasshoppers are about the only enemy of this plant. Insecticide spray will kill the small black baby ones, but the large yellow/red adults are more resistant. The best method is to hand-pick and crush them. Ugh!

Easter lily (*Lilium longiflorum*). Easter lilies are listed as one species in a large group known as Lilium, which includes tiger, madonna, and regal lilies. Blooming greenhouse-grown lilies are sold at Easter, but when grown in the ground in the South, they bloom somewhat later. After the blooms of container-grown specimens fade, plant them in the garden, and they will flower and multiply the following spring.

When planting bulbs, place at least three in a group. Groups of bulbs can be left undisturbed for years. New bulblets will form around the mother bulbs and will need to be divided (in the fall) when they become overcrowded.

Plant in the fall or early spring, covering bulbs to a depth of six inches. Unlike most bulbs, this type sends out roots from both the base of the bulb and from the stem. Easter lilies grow two to three feet tall and bear a cluster of six- to eight-inch white trumpet flowers on each stem. These lilies require moisture during the growing season but need good drainage. They do well when planted among perennials, in a groundcover, or among rocks, when their foliage gets full sun but their roots are shaded with mulch. Fertilize with a general balanced fertilizer in the fall and with a bulb fertilizer (4-8-8) as soon as they start to grow in the spring. Withhold fertilizer after the blooming period.

It is best to remove spent flowers before seeds can form, but don't remove foliage growth until it turns brown because this will weaken the plant and decrease future flowering.

Ginger lily (*Zingiber* spp.). This family of herbaceous perennials covers a large group of four hundred species that vary considerably in appearance. Varieties most often seen in the subtropics are Shell flower, Butterfly, Pine cone, Spiral flag, and Torch. These varieties are grown for their glossy, linear leaves and colorful flower spikes, not for edible roots. Commercial ginger (*Zingiber officinale*) is sometimes called Jamaica ginger. It has yellow-green cones with yellow-green and purple flowers. The tuberous roots are harvested and cured for making various ginger products.

Gingers are easy to grow, have few enemies, and—once established—require little care. They grow rapidly from rhizomes that crawl underground and send up new shoots from time to time.

Gingers that grow tall can serve as background plantings, screens, or accent clumps and can soften and add interest to corners or a blank wall. They are especially appealing near fresh water. The smaller varieties are used as edging plants or as accent plants in containers. They add tropical elegance to the landscape. Some species of ginger are used to make paper, and the leaf sheaths are a source of fiber for making rope.

Prime growing conditions are full morning sun or broken, shifting shade. They grow in a wide range of soil types, from sand to rich humus, as long as they receive adequate moisture. Gingers will tolerate some drought and neglect. Some varieties will grow in boggy soil or on the edges of ponds, lakes, or streams. They need to be protected from salt spray.

Planting, transplanting, or dividing clumps should be done in spring or fall. Remove soil to expose the rhizome and use a sharp knife or spade to cut them into pieces, making certain that each piece has at least one bud to produce a new plant. Set rhizomes not more than two to three inches below soil level. Fertilize with 6-6-6 in early spring when growth begins, again in midsummer, and yet again in the fall. Canes that have flowered should be cut off just above ground level as soon as the foliage begins to appear unattractive.

A mulch of partially decomposed compost will help hold moisture and protect the rhizomes in the event of a freeze. All of the gingers I have mentioned are somewhat freeze-tolerant. Although they may freeze down, they come back from the roots in the spring.

Shell flower ginger (*Alpinia* spp.) is the largest ginger genus and has many species. Bright green lanceolate leaves line each side of straight stalks that bear flowers from their terminal ends. Like a strand of closely strung shells, the white buds have a thin porcelain-like texture and are tipped in bright pink. They droop in a cluster from the ends of the leaf stalks. The buds open one at a time, and a fragrant flower pushes out. Each exquisite blossom, resembling a delicate seashell, is white with ruffled edges tinged in yellow, with red veins. A smaller shell flower ginger in southern Florida has crimson blossoms.

Alpinia variegata is a species in this family that is grown for its spectacular variegated (green and yellow) foliage. The bloom is insignificant, and it is not cold-tolerant.

Butterfly ginger (*Hedychium* spp.), with its ethereal delicacy and the enchanting fragrance of its white blossoms, is a lovely plant that should be in every southern garden. The petals resemble a shimmering butterfly. During the warm months flowers appear several at a time at the terminal end of the lush, leafy stalks. The average height of the plants is about three feet, but when grown in water at the edge of ponds, they may get much taller.

Pine cone ginger (*Zingiber zerumbet*) was so named because plants bear flower heads that resemble pine cones on leafless stems. The flower heads are bright red when mature. Small white flowers emerge from mature cones one at a time as the cone oozes a sweet, sticky nectar that attracts ants and bees. This variety blooms in fall and winter. The stems that bear leaves grow to be three or more feet tall. The broad leaves of pine cone lilies are much admired for indoor decoration.

Spiral flag ginger (*Costus* spp.) got its name because its leaves are spirally arranged on stems that twist like a corkscrew as they grow taller. The leaf stalks are topped by a dense red-to-coral cone from three to four inches long. Small coral flowers emerge from the cone as it oozes sweet, sticky nectar. The blossoms appear during the warm summer months. Spiral flag gingers are propagated by division of clumps, separation of offshoots that form below the flower heads, and cut sections of the stem.

Torch ginger (*Nicolaia elatior*) is among the most vigorous and spectacular of the gingers. Plants can form huge clumps of tall, heavily foliated stems. Beautiful bright-red, waxy cones stand terminally on separate, leafless stems. The showy part of the head is composed of red or pink bracts beneath small red flowers. The season of maximum color is the fall. Propagation is by division of clumps or seedage.

Gladiolus (G. spp.). The bulbs of the gladiolus can be planted in Florida throughout the year. However, keep in mind that it takes about three months before plants flower, so don't count on blooms that could be destroyed by frost. Glads are easy to grow if you start with healthy corms, choose a planting site in full sun, prepare the soil properly, and water adequately.

Glads are available in many types, sizes, and colors—from tiny species to giant blossoms, which include singles, doubles, ruffles, and fragrant.

Unlike many other bulbs, glads don't like extremely rich soil. The pH should be around 6, slightly acid. The soil must be loose so that it will drain well. The bulbs must be planted deep enough to hold up their heavy blossoms. Plant large bulbs six inches deep, smaller bulbs not so deep. The distance between bulbs will depend upon your plan for their use. If you are planting for color in your landscape, glads can be planted rather close together, about six inches apart. For cut flowers with large blossoms, plant in rows at least eight inches apart with two feet between rows. Mulch well. It's a good idea to change the planting site each year to avoid diseases in the soil.

When preparing bulbs for planting, carefully remove the loose outside skins. This makes the sprouting process easier and the stems straighter. Place corms with their buds up, but any that have already sprouted should have the sprout straight up regardless of the angle of the bulb. If there are several buds, you may want to cut off all but one or two in order to let the energy go toward larger, sturdier spikes and blossoms. When removing buds, dip the knife in a disinfectant between cuts and dust the cut areas with a fungicide. Cut corms should not be planted for several days until these surfaces have time to seal their wounds. For a prolonged period of bloom, plant some bulbs every two weeks.

Fertilize with a bulb fertilizer (4-8-8) about a month after planting and once each month thereafter. Stop just before flowers start to bloom. Water well at least once each week, depending upon rainfall.

The best time to cut the blossoms is when only two or three of the flowerlets at the bottom have opened. Leave about four inches of foliage to help the bulb mature for the next season.

It is best to dig glad bulbs and not allow them to winter in the ground. However, you don't have to wait until the foliage turns brown to dig the corms. Dig them about six weeks after they have bloomed and carefully clean them by placing them on a screen and hosing off the soil. Dip them in a fungicide and allow them to dry in the sun for about three weeks. Then twist off the old bulb and store, right side up, in boxes without lids. Dust with a pesticide and keep in a cool place until planting time.

Glads are sometimes left in the ground for two to three years before digging and dividing. If they are fortunate enough to have escaped pests and disease, dig and separate corms as they become too crowded and plant them in the fall or early spring months.

Glory lily (*Gloriosa rothschildiana* or *G. superba*). Grown from tubers, this vine climbs by tendrils on the ends of slender leaves. Each vine has several branches with many showy flowers. The flowers are very striking, with dainty ruffled petals that flare backward and stand up in a perky manner. They display bright colors. Rothschildiana has yellow petals turning scarlet, and superba has orange petals that darken to red. The plants emerge in late spring and continue to bloom throughout the summer. After the blooming period, the foliage turns yellow and dies down to the ground. Pull up the vine and discard it. Tubers will remain in the ground to come up the following spring, or they can be dug for relocation.

When planting tubers, lay them horizontally and place them four to five inches deep. The tubers are somewhat jointed and may be broken into pieces to start new vines. Several tubers can be planted in the same area to assure a large clump of vines with numerous flowers.

Glory vines need water, but the soil should drain well. Plant them in full sun. Fertilize with a balanced product when the new growth appears. Because tubers often travel underground, don't be surprised if they don't come up where you planted them or, in successive years, come up some distance away.

Blood lily (*Haemanthus multiflorus*). The blood lily produces a spectacular cluster of flowers on a single strong, leafless stalk in May or June. Its red flower mass may be as large as a grapefruit. Flower stalks appear before the leaves, making a rather strange bouquet. When flowers start to fade, three or four strap leaves appear at the base of the plant to supply nourishment for next year's bulbs.

The leaves are somewhat thin, eight to ten inches long, and grow on long stems. The stems are marked with reddish-brown spots. Blood lilies can be grown in pots or in the yard, but they seem to flower more freely when roots are confined. They can't survive frost, so pots should be taken indoors when necessary. On the other hand, they don't like full, hot sunshine and temperatures above eighty degrees. Morning sun is ideal.

Plant in spring or fall, and set the bulb so that its tip is just above the surface. It isn't necessary to dig the bulbs after they go dormant in the fall. Under ideal growing conditions they multiply rapidly into large clumps. When the clump gets large and blooms seem to be decreasing, dig, separate, and replant.

Fertilize three times a year—spring, summer, and fall—with a bulb fertilizer (4-8-8). During the dormant period in winter, withhold fertilizer and ease up on water so that the bulbs can rest. If your bulbs are growing in the yard, mark the spot so they won't be disturbed.

Blood lily flowers set seed about the size of a large pea that becomes red when ripe. Bulbs grown from seed may take three years to bloom. You can also propagate them by removing small bulbs that form around the mother bulb.

Day lily (*Hemerocallis* spp.). Members of the rhizome class, day lilies have long been popular garden subjects due to their hardiness, ease of maintenance, and wide selection of colors. They are excellent seaside plants. Selective breeding of species has produced many distinctive varieties that number in the thousands. Day lily growers are enthusiastic gardeners, and many belong to local hemerocallis societies and the American Hemerocallis Society to share knowledge, experience, and plants.

Varieties of these herbaceous perennials bloom from early spring until late fall. They can be planted and transplanted at almost anytime if given the proper care until established. September is considered an ideal time in central Florida for planting new rhizomes or dividing old clumps. Fall planting gives the plant a rest period after the blooming season, and the bulbs have time to manufacture and store food for next year's growth.

Day lilies are classified into three groups according to their growth habits: deciduous, semi-evergreen, and evergreen. Evergreen day lilies do best in warmer climates.

Plants and flowers are available in various sizes to fit your landscape plans. These colorful plants have many landscape uses but are most effective when used with an evergreen background and in combination with other flowers. They need to show off their colors when blooming but disguise their foliage as it starts to fade in the fall.

Colors range from yellow, gold, and orange to pink and purple and shades of brown, mahogany, and burgundy. Careful consideration should be given to color selection in order to keep flowers in harmony with each other, other plants, and the color of your home. Plant ten or more plants of the same color in informal groupings or three or more in bays of informal shrubbery. For a striking border, stagger two rows of miniature plants in one color or a combination of complementary colors. Tall varieties look charming when peeping over the top of a wall.

Under central Florida conditions, day lily plants are allowed to grow for five to ten years in one location. The rate of multiplication depends on the growth rate, which is based on growing conditions. Therefore, it is very important to prepare the planting bed properly. These perennials grow best in rich, well-drained soil. Set plants twelve to eighteen inches apart on a slight mound of soil. Spread roots to the outer area of the mound and cover with soil, tamping lightly. Mulch plants generously. Water with a fine spray to a depth of one inch, and continue doing so twice a week until roots are well established. After that, day lilies are easily maintained and relatively free from insects and disease. Aphids or chewing insects can be a problem but can be controlled by spraying with the correct pesticide.

Fertilize at least twice a year in early spring and midsummer using a balanced organic fertilizer (6-6-6). Apply to the soil around plants but not on the foliage. Day lilies can tolerate some drought conditions but should be watered well after fertilizing.

Propagation is by seed or division. When the clumps get so crowded that the flower production is reduced, it is time to divide. To divide, dig up the clumps with a large, sharp knife; sever the rhizome between the fans of leaves; and then cut the leaves back to within four inches of the crown. Replant divisions in the soil one inch deeper than the junction of roots and foliage. To start new plants, cut rhizomes any place between buds.

Paper-white narcissus (*Narcissus tazetta*). An old favorite highly recommended for the southeast, narcissus bloom in January and February when flowers are scarce. They are exceptionally free of the insects and diseases that spell disaster to some bulbs. Narcissus make excellent cut flowers with their many small crowned blossoms growing on one upright stem. They last several days indoors if picked when only half of the flowers in a cluster have opened. This species has white petals with white or yellow cups and is very fragrant. The thin strap leaves grow about twelve inches long in a clump around the flower stems.

Paper-white narcissus can be planted at any time, but for January bloom should be planted in September. Soil should be only moderately fertile. Separate crowded clumps, and replant bulbs about every five years. Plant bulbs four inches deep and about eight inches apart in beds arranged in groupings or scattered about in a natural way. Narcissus are especially attractive in rock gardens. Full sun or high shade is best. Fertilize lightly with a general or bulb fertilizer once or twice a year after a blooming period. Don't overfertilize or you'll have lush foliage and few flowers. If this should happen, dig the bulbs and give them a rest until fall planting time.

If you wish to dig your bulbs, wait until after the foliage has turned yellow and has had time to store up nourishment for next year's blossoms. Remove the baby bulbs and replant right away. Place the mature bulbs in a shallow box until they dry out. Then remove the dead tops, dust with a pesticide, and keep in a cool place until planting time in the fall. It may take two years before baby bulbs flower.

Moderate moisture and freedom from weeds during growing periods are their only demands. Cold winters—after blooming period—are welcomed. When bulbs have a chance to go dormant and rest, they flower more abundantly.

Rain lily, zephyr lily (*Zephyranthes* spp.). These warm-weather bulbs usher in the rainy season with their soft white, pink, or rose single flowers. The summer rains magically bring out the blooms for several weeks, and the bulbs are not fooled by irrigation water. Rain lilies are easy to propagate and adapt well to new environments.

Wet, sunny conditions are best, but rain lilies will tolerate some drought and broken, shifting shade. Bulbs should be set two inches deep and about three inches apart in well-drained soil. They do best in moderately fertile soil, and the thin strap leaves appreciate fertilization (6-6-6 or 4-8-8) once a year in the spring.

Rain lily blossoms leave a pod that contains many seeds, which are scattered by the wind. They will come up in the lawn in lovely patches. The bulbs multiply so rapidly that after several seasons it may be necessary to dig, separate, and replant. New plants from baby bulbs may bloom their first year.

Society garlic (*Tulbaghia violacea*). These bulbous roots are popular throughout the South because they require very little care, bloom constantly during the warm months, and will tolerate some salt air. The violet flowers bloom in clusters on leafless stalks. The thin strap leaves are almost a foot long and give off a garlic scent when crushed. Society garlic has small bulbs that are easy to plant and transplant.

Society garlic can be planted anytime of the year in the South. Set the bulbs about eight inches apart because they multiply rapidly. Their growth habit produces a mass of tangled roots, making it necessary to dig, separate into small clumps, and replant every four to five years. When the plants stop blooming, you will know that it is time to dig and replant. Propagate from the small bulbs that develop around large ones. Plant in full sun for the most blossoms. Keep moist and fertilize with a general balanced product (6-6-6) spring, summer, and fall. The foliage may be damaged by frost, but new growth will soon appear.

TULIPS (*Tulipa* SPP.)

Some degree of success may be possible with growing tulips in the warmer parts of Florida if they are grown as annuals. If the bulbs are left in the ground, some may come up the following year, but chances are they won't bloom. Bulbs you order by mail probably haven't been refrigerated to allow a period of dormancy. Here is the procedure to follow: Order the bulbs around the first of October. As soon as you receive them, place them loosely in a brown paper bag (not plastic). Put the bag in the vegetable drawer of your refrigerator. Be sure the bulbs are dry, and keep the bag dry while in the refrigerator. Dampness will cause fungus and the bulbs will rot. After eight to twelve weeks, plant the bulbs in the morning sun or high shade. Failure to provide proper storage may not show up when the bulbs produce foliage but will prevent them from blooming.

POINSETTIAS

U.S. residents have adopted the showy poinsettia as a symbol of winter festivities. It has become a cash crop for growers and shippers during late fall and early winter. Each year there are new hybrids and innovative ways of planting them in containers.

Plan to have the cheerful poinsettia among your plants when the days shorten and the weather keeps us indoors. Its bright color will warm up a gloomy day.

Description

Poinsettias belong to the Spurge family, genus *Euphorbia pulcherrima* (Latin for "very beautiful"). They are listed as flowering shrubs with large, medium-to-dark green leaves. The sap is milky. The true flowers are small, yellow, cup-shaped structures in the center of a swirl of brightly colored, modified leaves called bracts. These bracts generally start to develop in October.

The original bracts were single and red, but hybridizers have developed double and triple varieties in red, white, cream, pink, pink peppermint, lemon drop, marble, and variegated. The newer ones have stronger stems, are more tolerant to temperature changes, and have longer-lasting blooms.

Innovative places to grow poinsettias include hanging baskets, all sizes of pots and tubs, and strawberry jars. They may also be grown as trees or topiaries. The containers may contain single or multiple plants. Many varieties are available as are mini and maxi sizes.

History

The poinsettia is thought to have originated as a wild flower in a limited region south of Mexico City near the present town of Taxco. The Aztecs had cultivated it long before the arrival of Europeans. During the seventeenth century, Franciscan friars from Spain settled in the area. When they found the bright flower blooming during the season of Advent, they used it to adorn the nativity celebration and called it "the flower of the Holy Night."

Used to decorate homes and churches in Mexico during the Christmas season, this exotic plant was introduced to the United States by Dr. Joel Poinsett. Returning from his term of office as U.S. ambassador to Mexico, he brought the plants home to his native South Carolina. The plant was named in his honor.

Characteristics

These plants are known as photoperiod bloomers. This means that they respond to the changing length of nature's light periods (long night/short day). Poinsettias are temperamental during the flower-setting period. Total darkness at night is essential for them to bloom fully. Any stray light during this period will disrupt or delay the flowering process.

Poinsettias are not salt-tolerant or cold-hardy. In the event of a freeze, do not dig your plants. Many times they can be cut back to live wood, or to the ground, and they will send up new growth in the spring.

Growing Requirements

Poinsettias will grow satisfactorily in a wide range of well-drained soils. Place outdoors in full sunlight, preferably on the south or west side of the house with something serving as a windbreak. About three times a year, in March, June, and September, apply a complete fertilizer in which nitrogen, phosphorus, and potash are balanced (6-6-6 or 8-8-8). The amount of fertilizer will depend upon the age and size of your plants.

Pruning and Propagation

Outdoor plants are generally pruned about three times each year: during spring, again in summer, and not later than the middle of August. This will depend upon how tall you wish your plants to be at Christmastime. Pruning promotes branching and thus more bracts and more color. Pruning later than mid-August will delay color, and your plants may not have time to become pretty for the holidays. These plants grow rapidly. Vigorous, healthy plants will grow about three feet in height in the three months following the mid-August pruning.

Healthy hardwood cuttings can be used to start new plants. They root easily. Dip the cut end of six- to eight-inch cuttings into a rooting hormone. Then insert about three-quarters of the stem into sandy soil and keep moist.

Ten Steps for Success with Houseplant Poinsettias

The following ten points are based on suggestions from America's foremost poinsettia breeder—the Paul Ecke Poinsettia Ranch, Box 488, Encinitas, California 92024.

1. Select plants with green foliage all the way down to the soil line. This is a good indication that the plants have active, healthy roots.

2. Look for plants that have small green buttons in the center of the colored bracts. These buttons will develop into little yellow flowers. Fully opened flowers indicate an older plant that will most probably not stay fresh and pretty as long.

3. When transporting the plants, make sure they are protected from temperatures below fifty degrees. Chilling causes leaf drop. Be careful not to bump the foliage because the stems are brittle and break easily. A good way to transport your poinsettia plants is to use a cardboard box turned upside down with a hole cut in the bottom to match the size of your pot.

4. Place plants in a room where there is sufficient natural light. These plants need at least six hours of bright, indirect light daily to do well. Keep away from drafts and hot-air registers.

5. Water plants thoroughly when you get them home. Remove any foil wrap, or punch a hole in the bottom, to allow good drainage. Thoroughly saturate the soil until water seeps through the drain hole in the bottom of the pot. Plants must not sit in water.

6. Check plants daily, and water only when the soil feels dry. Over-watering will kill your plants. This is very important!

7. Fertilize within several days. These plants are without nutrients during the marketing process and will need to be fed. It is best to use liquid plant fertilizer, following the directions on the label.

8. To prolong the bright color of the bracts, don't allow the temperature to exceed seventy-two degrees during the day and sixty degrees at night.

9. If your plants deteriorate after the holidays, prune them back, leaving two or three leaf nodes per stem. Set them near a window and keep them slightly moist. When the weather warms up, they will develop new shoots. Newer varieties will stay pretty for several months. Cut them back only after they start to lose their beauty.

10. In the spring you may transplant them to slightly larger containers or place them in the yard. Choose a location that is away from artificial light, protected from the wind, and

receives at least six hours of sun each day. Poinsettias will grow in a wide range of soils with an application of a general fertilizer (6-6-6 or 8-8-8) three times a year (spring, June, and late September).

Poinsettias as Cut Flowers

Poinsettias were popular as fresh cut flowers long before they were grown as potted plants. The secret is to treat the stems in order to coagulate the milky sap and thus reduce wilt. There are a number of ways to accomplish this.

Be sure your cutting tool is sharp enough to make a clean cut. Immediately immerse the cut end of the stem in moderately hot water for about one minute. Then place in cool water. Use care to prevent the hot water from damaging the bracts and flowers.

Or you can quickly singe the cut end of the stem over a flame as soon as it is cut and then place the stem in cool tap water (not ice).

Use a floral preservative in the vase water. This can be a commercial preservative, or you can make one by using two teaspoons of a 10 percent solution of liquid chlorine bleach per gallon of water. Be sure to replace the water every few days with a fresh solution.

Keep flowers out of direct sunlight. Place in an area where the temperature is mild and there is good air circulation. Do not refrigerate. With proper care, the bracts should last from seven to ten days.

Poinsettias should be cut at least eighteen to twenty-four hours before they are used in arrangements.

Mass arrangements of one color, or a combination of two or more colors, are effective and eye-catching.

HIBISCUS

No plant can give the illusion of a tropical environment quite as well as the beautiful, colorful blooms of the hibiscus. They come in every color—solids, blends, and combinations. They may be miniature or as large as a dinner plate. Whether single, double, scalloped, ruffled, fringed, or plain, all hibiscus are entrancing. The blooms of most varieties lasts only one day, but the following morning another flower will take its place. There are a few newer hybrids that will last two or more days, especially in a cool environment. Blossoms placed in a refrigerator will remain open overnight.

Every garden should be graced with a few hibiscus plants. They are inexpensive, easy to plant, easy to grow, and require very little maintenance. They will brighten any corner where you are!

Description

This woody perennial (*Hibiscus rosa-sinensis*) is a close relative of cotton, okra, rose-of-Sharon, mallow, Confederate rose, and roselle (Florida cranberry). There are so many varieties of hibiscus that they defy counting. If you purchase a hibiscus and it blooms with dramatic flowers ten to twelve inches across, don't get excited! You were sold a mallow—a cousin of the hibiscus.

Hibiscus grow prolifically in tropical climates throughout the world but are said to be indigenous to China, India, and the Pacific Islands. According to American Hibiscus Society historians, great strides were made in these ornamental plants in the early eighteenth century. Much later, they became popular in America.

Generally, *Hibiscus rosa-sinensis* is a woody shrub, but the genus also exists in tree form. Two especially interesting species of hibiscus are the mahoe (*H. elatus*), a stunning tree whose flowers appear yellow in the morning, orange in the afternoon, and bright red in the evening; and a small tree form, the Confederate rose (*H. mutabilis*), which blooms snow-white in the morning and turns a delicate apple-blossom pink in the afternoon.

Hibiscus foliage is a lovely, shiny, dark green when in good health; the leaves may also be variegated. The leaves may appear ovate (egg-shaped) to cordate (heart-shaped) and almost any shape in between. The foliage is not salt-tolerant on the oceanfront, but more robust varieties do well from the second dune line with protection from winds.

No water is required to keep hibiscus flowers fresh after they are picked. This makes them valuable for corsages, garlands, leis, or centerpieces. They do bruise easily, so they must be handled with care.

Besides their showiness as ornamentals and cut flowers, hibiscus have some other interesting uses: as ingredients for boot black, mascara, and perfume; as the base for a variety of teas; and as a jelly. In China, the leaf was once used as a vegetable, and the flower is still sometimes minced to garnish salads.

Propagation

Propagating new plants from cuttings is very easy. A mature plant can be grown from a healthy cutting in less than a year.

Keep all dead wood removed from hibiscus and groom each plant to the size and shape you desire. Use green wood cuttings from pruning for propagation. Root in water in a clear glass container and then plant, or apply a rooting hormone to the cut end of your cutting and plant in loose potting soil, or air-layer terminals of the mother plant. Plants grafted on healthy stock grow more vigorously and produce the most beautiful flowers, but this technique requires special knowledge. See the section on propagation in chapter 1.

Hibiscus plants produce seeds in a pod as the flowers fade. These pods split as they mature, and the seeds may be planted to produce new plants. However, this method of propagation is very slow.

One of the interesting things about planting seeds is that you never can be sure what you're going to get. You may have a dozen seeds from a single pod, but no two seedlings produce an identical plant. This has created a problem because many inferior strains have been encouraged to develop.

Cross-pollination to produce a new flower is a popular pursuit of hibiscus growers. They select two different blooms and cross their pollens, which may produce a new type. This is one reason for the large number of different varieties. These varieties are often named for wives, husbands, or girlfriends or for something that describes a plant's appearance.

Growing Hibiscus

Hibiscus are easy to grow and with a minimum of care will produce a succession of colorful displays almost every month of the year. They are fast growing, and the requirements are uncomplicated. They need regular watering in well-drained soil. Overwatering will turn the leaves yellow and eventually kill the plant. Hibiscus are tolerant of a variety of soil conditions, but the standard soil formula recommended for planting consists of one-third peat (compost), one-third cow manure, and one-third topsoil. Later, during the growing months, a good general garden fertilizer (6-6-6) once each month should be adequate. These plants do best in a soil with a pH range of 6.5 to 7. Although hibiscus will flourish in partial shade, full sun will produce more blossoms.

Precautions for Growing Hibiscus

Climate. Temperature is the most crucial requirement for these plants. They are at their best in temperatures ranging from sixty to ninety degrees. Lower temperatures may cause the loss of leaves and a dormant state. Young plants can be killed by frost, but mature, strong plants will usually come back from the root system. Higher temperatures can burn buds or brown the edges of the leaves.

When they need winter protection from frost and cold winds, plants in containers should be brought indoors or put into a heated greenhouse. Smaller plants in the ground can be dug, put into pots, and brought inside. Larger plants can be banked with soil twelve to fifteen inches around the stalk and covered with large cardboard cartons. Soil banked around the plants can be left all winter.

Cold weather dehydrates plants; therefore, they must be watered well when a freeze is predicted and before you cover them. If frost gets on plants, they can sometimes be saved if you hose it off before the sun hits the foliage.

Control of pests. There are few insect and disease problems associated with growing hibiscus. Spraying is generally unnecessary unless spider mites, aphids, or worms appear. The foliage of hibiscus plants is delicate and can be severely damaged by pesticide sprays. Get advice from a reliable nursery.

Mulch plants to conserve moisture and control weeds. Keep the mulch material, whether leaves, pine straw, grass clippings, or partially decomposed compost, away from the trunk of the plant in order to prevent fungus and insect invasion of the bark.

Take time to smell the flowers.

Redbud blossoms alert us to the fact that spring is on the way.

Golden rain trees offer golden showers of blossoms in September.

The coral pods of golden rain trees soften the sky in October.

Formosa azaleas are Florida's hardiest and grow the largest. They bloom in March and April.

Bromeliads rate high among our most interesting flowering plants.

Above: Geraniums are a Florida tradition—and an American classic.

Right: Cucumbers, "the patrons of the pickle jar," are displayed here with garlic and dill.

Left: Roses are known as "the queen of flowers."

Below: A patio can be a lovely extension to any home.

Above: Amaryllis rank
high in the bulb world.

Left: Canna lilies offer
bright colors for back-
ground planting.

Fragrant paper-white narcissus usher in the New Year.

Poinsettias say, "Merry Christmas."

Left: Ardisias add variety to the Christmas season.

Below: Portulacas are lovely for hanging baskets, rock gardens, or groundcovers.

Above: A traditional favorite in white or lavender, wisteria blossoms are a harbinger of spring.

Right: Bring in some holiday cheer from the garden.

Left: The glossy leaves and golden trumpets of allamanda can be trained as a vine or a shrub.

Below: Fragrant, cascading nasturtiums offer a riot of color.

The graceful arching fronds of the holly fern make it an ideal container plant.

Single, double, frilled, or fringed, hibiscus plants are a tropical favorite.

Left: Hollyhocks lend elegance and dignity.

Below: Turn your rock wall into a flower garden.

Above: Raised beds can be a great way to garden.

Right: Shasta, gaillardia, and coneflower daisies make cheerful companions.

Top: Majestic Beauty, a variety of India hawthorn, is perfectly named.

Above left: Create a delightful butterfly garden.

Above right: Shell ginger (*Alpinia zerumbet*) has fragrant pendulous clusters that resemble delicate seashells.

Right: Butterfly ginger (*Hedychium flavum*) is aptly named and has a delightful fragrance.

Moonbeam coreopsis sends its soft rays over the garden all summer long.

Slow-growing and long-lived, the Rhaphis palms are adaptable plants for interiors as well as southern exteriors. Shown here is the dwarf lady palm (*R. excelsa*).

Sea oats (*Uniola paniculata*) anchor the sand dunes and enhance a lovely view of the ocean.

Seaside sunflowers (*Helianthus debilis*) are excellent sand binders and display bright little faces almost all year round.

Hardy Shrubs

Two general rules pertain to the shrubs discussed in this section. After the plants are well established and seem to be thriving, they will need to be fertilized only twice a year—in March and September or October. All will require watching for the invasion of common pests such as thrips, aphids, spider mites, worms, mealybugs, caterpillars, grasshoppers, and beetles. Spray as necessary.

Favorite Varieties of Shrubs

Christmas berry (*Ardisia crenata*). This dwarf shrub will tolerate salt in the air if protected from direct wind and spray from the ocean. It has beautiful dark green, glossy leaves with tiny scalloped edges, bearing white or pink flowers followed by large red berries for the Christmas season. Therefore, it is worth some extra attention. Plant in a planter protected from direct salt drift. Rinse the foliage with clear water from time to time. Ardisia grows well in high shade in fertile, acid soil. If frozen to ground level, it will come back from the roots.

Euonymus (*E. fortunei*). There doesn't seem to be an overall common name for this handsome landscape shrub, which thrives in sun or partial shade. There are many varieties—three-foot dwarfs, four- to six-foot plants for accents and hedges, and six- to fifteen-foot shrubs for backgrounds. Euonymus responds well to pruning but requires very little. Most varieties keep their leaves year round in the southern part of the United States. These plants are available with all green foliage or variegated with green and white or green and yellow. The foliage is subject to powdery mildew and scale. Euonymus plants do well in average soil and are salt-tolerant back from the first dune line.

Fatsia (*F. japonica*). This shrub has broad, deep-lobed leaves held up by thick green stems that present an oriental effect, similar in appearance to the rice-paper plant. The white flowers are insignificant, but fatsia foliage makes an excellent landscape or indoor plant. It doesn't like full sun but thrives in reduced light areas. Fatsia has a moderate tolerance for salt spray and will spring back up in a few days after being weighted down by ice from a heavy frost. Fatsia needs fertile soil, compost, and moist soil.

Firethorn (*Pyracantha coccinea*). This sprawling shrub has vicious thorny branches that produce clusters of small, showy white flowers in spring. Numerous berries follow and turn bright orange or red in late fall. Firethorn can be trained as a vine, espaliered, or kept trimmed as a shrub or small tree. It requires rather extensive pruning each year in late winter. Plants grow best in full sun, back from the front dune lines, and will thrive in relatively poor, sandy soil.

India hawthorn (*Rhaphiolepis* spp.). There are many varieties, ranging from a dwarf shrub to a tree about twelve feet tall. The leaves are dark green and leathery. The size of the leaves is determined by the species. Tree hawthorns have very large leaves. Small clusters of white, rose, or pink flowers appear in spring, summer, and fall. India hawthorn is an excellent seaside plant in full sun or partial shade. It is tolerant of wind, salt spray, and some drought conditions but needs fertile soil.

Juniper (*Juniperus* spp.). There are many species of these coniferous shrubs—columnar, dwarf, tree, creeping groundcover, or a shrub of any size. There is one to serve almost every purpose. They do well in hot or cold climates, dry or wet conditions, good soil or rocky ledges, and near the beach. Foliage varies with species—dark green, blue-green, gray-green, and golden-yellow. Maintenance is minimal. Junipers lend themselves well to pruning if done skillfully. Their worst enemy is the spider mite. If caught early, these mites can be eradicated with a pesticide spray; if not, they can kill the plant.

Ligustrum (*L. lucidum, japonicum,* and *sinense*). These three species of ligustrum are the ones used most often in the Southeast. They all belong to the privet family and are evergreens. Lucidum and japonicum start as small shrubs; but when overgrown, they can be pruned to make charming trees with interesting trunks and limbs. They have glossy, dark green—or marbled with yellow—leaves and terminal panicles of fragrant white flowers in the spring followed by blue-black fruits in the fall. Ligustrum thrive in full sun or partial shade in widely varying soils. They can withstand frost of short duration and salt spray if planted as far back from the ocean as the third dune line. There are almost no problems with insects and diseases.

Natal plum (*Carissa* spp.). This shrub comes in tree or dwarf varieties. The leaves are a glossy dark green and grow in a dense, compact manner. Beautiful, fragrant white flowers are followed by scarlet, plumlike fruit. Stout thorns help protect the fruit from the birds. The fruit is very decorative, matures year round, and makes delicious jelly. Carissa are ideal oceanfront plants, making good barriers, accents, and foundation plantings. They like full sun best and are tolerant of salt and sandy soils.

Pittosporum (*P. tobira*). This plant has many varieties, from dwarf to fifteen feet tall, which are used for foundation, accent, or hedge plants. Thick clustered stems bearing whorled, revolute, leathery, green or variegated leaves produce small, fragrant white flowers in the spring. Pittosporum will grow in sun or shade but must have fertile, slightly acid, well-drained soil. They require more attention than most other shrubs listed in this chapter. If mulch, fertilizer, and water are not adequately supplied, the leaves lose their luster, scales attack, and the roots develop fungus root rot. Pittosporum have excellent tolerance to salt and are good seaside plants.

Plumbago (*P. capensis*). Plumbago is an extremely popular dwarf flowering shrub, useful as a transition plant, a foundation plant, a hedge, or in a planter. It can be trained as a vine when planted near a support. Clusters of white or blue flowers are produced during much of the year. The flowers produce a sweet, sticky nectar loved by butterflies and hummingbirds. Small capsules that cling like burrs develop as the blossoms fade. The foliage is light green, fine-textured, and evergreen. Plumbago grows rapidly on sprawling branches and should be pruned to control size and shape after each flush of bloom fades. Pruning promotes strong new growth and more flowers. These plants tolerate a wide range of soils but do best in fertile soil with good drainage. Plant in full sun for best growth and flowering. Plumbago will tolerate salt drift behind the second dune line. This shrub is relatively insect-free except for cottony cushion scale and mites.

Podocarpus (*P.* spp.). Podocarpus species belong to the large yew family. The many species range from small shrubs to thirty-foot trees. The flat evergreen leaves may be fine to broad and are heavily foliated on firm stems. Some species make nice espalier plants. Old foliage is dark green, and the new growth is silvery. Flowers are inconspicuous but develop edible red fruit that can be made into delicious jelly. The yew family needs fertile, well-drained soil in sun or shade. They are tolerant of salt drift behind the front dunes.

Prickly pear cactus (*Opuntia* spp.). There are several species of this plant grown in Florida right on the first dune line. They bloom prolifically in spring and summer. Flowers, borne on the upper margins of flat pads, are red, yellow, purple, or white and are very showy. Flowers are followed by juicy edible fruits that are generally purple in color. They are served as a delicacy in some restaurants in Florida. Like most cacti, prickly pears thrive best in full sun and well-drained sandy soil.

Propagation is easy by breaking off a joint and sticking it into the ground. These plants are practically pest-free. This could be partly due to the fact that the foliage is covered with spines and fine bristles, which are perilous to human beings.

Rice-paper plant (*Tetrapanax papyriferus*). This is often planted in Florida for its evergreen, tropical foliage. The lobed leaves can be from one to three feet wide. Tall panicles of creamy-white flowers appear in spring and the warm months. A group of plants is truly a spectacular scene at blooming time. The leaves are furry underneath and can cause allergic reactions to human beings. Plants are killed to the ground by frost but, being rapid growers, come back from the roots in the spring. Unfortunately, these plants are invasive and can become a nuisance if not kept under control. They propagate by suckers that appear underground or by many seeds blown from the blossoms.

Rice-paper plants will thrive in full sun or partial shade and in poor soil. They will tolerate salt spray back from the first dune line.

The common name of these plants derives from the fact that the stems are used for making rice paper in Asia.

Silverthorn (*Elaeagnus* spp.). The silverthorn is available as a dwarf, a regular shrub, or a vine. It's a rapid grower with sprawling, reaching, thorny canes, so it should be planted in spacious areas unless pruned often. The bark is scruffy. Its leaves have tiny brown dots on top with silver undersides, which are lovely when waving in the breeze. Small brown flowers emerge in winter followed by small brown fruit. Silverthorn shrubs are tolerant of salt, drought, wind, and poor soil. They prefer full sun or light shade.

Wax myrtle (*Myrica cerifera*). Native to Florida, the myrtles have small, serrated, waxy, dark green leaves. They are robust and can be kept low or allowed to grow into small trees. Inconspicuous white flowers are followed by waxy, grayish-green berries in autumn. Berry drop can be a problem. Myrtles thrive in full sun or partial shade and do well in either poor, dry, wet, or rich soil. They are tolerant of salt drift, wind, and cold. Wax myrtles are superior plants for screens, windbreaks, or accent areas. They are not ideal for hedges because the foliage has a tendency to become sparse toward the ground as plants mature.

HARDY TREES

We have taken trees for granted throughout the years. You might ask, "Why not? Aren't there all kinds of trees everywhere we look?" The answer depends upon where you happen to look. In fact, the demolishing of trees has become a critical situation.

This book emphasizes the planting of trees because of their importance to our environment. In populated areas, much responsibility for that planting lies with the homeowner. We must hurry because we are far behind. Today, more trees are being destroyed than being planted.

We need trees for many reasons. They help clean our air and supply oxygen; serve as sound, dust, wind, and heat pollution shields; provide privacy and conceal unsightliness by serving as screens; lower temperatures by providing shade and by evaporation of water from their leaves; reduce soil erosion; help take care of surface water; attract birds and squirrels; and serve as an essential building material. All of these things also contribute to an increase in the value of your property.

This section deals only with those trees that have proven to be hardy along the Florida coastline.

Table 1. Hardy trees and their principal characteristics

	Mature height (ft.)	Native	Type	Growth	Nutrition
Apple	15	N	D	F	H
Bay, loblolly	50	Y	E	Mod	L
Bay, red	30	Y	E	Sl	L
Buckeye	60	Y	D	Mod	L
Camphor	50	Y	E	F	L
Cedar, red	35	Y	E	F	L
Cherry-laurel	40	Y	E	F	L
Chinese tallow	30	N	D	Mod	Mod
Crape myrtle	20	N	D	Mod	Mod
Cypress	80	Y	D	Sl	L
Dogwood	35	Y	D	Sl	Mod
Elm[1]	40	N	D	F	L
Eucalyptus	80	N	E	F	L
Hickory	80	Y	D	Sl	L
Loquat	20	N	E	F	Mod
Magnolia	80	Y	E	Sl	Mod
Maple	75	Y	D	F	L
Mimosa	30	N	D	F	Mod
Oak[2]	45	Y	E	Mod	L
Peach	18	N	D	Mod	H
Persimmon	20	N	D	Mod	H
Pine[3]	80	Y	E	Sl	L
Redbud	40	Y	D	Mod	L
Sumac	20	Y	D	Mod	L
Sycamore	80	Y	D	F	L
Sweet gum	80	Y	D	Mod	L
Wax myrtle	20	Y	E	F	L

[1]Elms: Chinese, Drake, weeping.

[2]Oaks: laurel, live, water.

[3]Pines: slash, sand.

Key: D = deciduous; H = high; O = obscure; S = sun; E = evergreen; L = low, not showy; T = tender; F = fast; Mod = moderate; R = rich; V = variable; Hdy = hardy; N = no; Sl = slow; Y = yes.

Flowering	Sun	Soil	Drought tolerance	Frost tolerance	Salt tolerance
Y	S	R	Mod	Hdy	N
Y	V	R	N	Hdy	N
O	V	V	Y	Hdy	Y
Y	V	V	Mod	Hdy	N
O	S	V	Y	Hdy	Mod
O	V	V	Y	Hdy	Mod
Y	V	V	Y	Hdy	Y
Y	S	V	Y	Hdy	N
Y	S	V	Y	Hdy	N
O	V	R	N	Hdy	N
Y	V	R	Y	Hdy	N
O	S	V	Y	Hdy	N
Y	S	V	Y	T	Y
O	S	V	Y	Hdy	N
O	S	V	Y	Hdy	Mod
Y	S	V	Y	Hdy	Y
O	S	V	N	Hdy	Mod
Y	S	V	Y	Hdy	N
O	S	V	Y	Hdy	Y
Y	S	R	Y	Hdy	N
Y	S	R	Mod	Hdy	N
O	S	V	Y	Hdy	Mod
Y	V	R	Y	Hdy	N
O	S	V	Y	Hdy	Mod
O	S	V	Y	Hdy	Mod
O	S	V	Y	Hdy	N
O	V	V	Y	Hdy	Y

Table 2. Flowering trees and their principal characteristics

Tree	Flower	Season
Apple	White, pink	Spring
Banana shrub	Cream, very fragrant	Spring
Bay, loblolly	White	Spring–summer
Bottle brush	Pink, red, rust	Summer
Camellia	Many shades/variegated	December–January
Candlebush	Golden yellow	Fall–winter
Cherry laurel	White	March
Chinaberry	Pale blue	Summer
Citrus	Fragrant white	March–April
Crape myrtle	White, pink, red, purple	Summer
Dogwood	White, pink	Spring
Firethorn	White flowers	April
followed by	red/orange berries	November–March
Gardenia	White	May
Golden rain	Yellow flowers	September–November
followed by	coral pods	October–November
India hawthorn	White, pink	Spring–summer
Jacaranda	Lavender	April–June
Jerusalem thorn	Yellow	Spring–Summer
Ligustrum	White	March
Magnolia	White	April–June
Maple	Rosy red	January–February
Mimosa	Shades of pink	Spring–summer
Natal plum	White bloom	
followed by	red fruit	Year round
Oleander	Reds, cream, white, yellow	Summer–late fall
Orchid[1]	Purple, red, white	Summer–fall[2]
Papaya	Cream	Summer–fall
Peach	White, pink	March
Pear	White	March
Redbud	Purple	Early spring
Royal poinciana	Red, yellow	Spring–summer
Schefflera	Red	June–August
Silk oak	Orange to rust	Spring–summer
Wild hog plum	White	February–March

Note: Plants that bear colorful berries or nuts for show and as food for birds and squirrels include ardesia, camphor, cedar, cherry laurel, cypress, dogwood, firethorn, hickory, holly, magnolia, mulberry, oak, pecan, pine, podocarpus, and wax myrtle. All flowering plants bloom best in full sun.

Type	Tolerance to	
	Frost	Salt
Deciduous	Hardy	No
Evergreen	Hardy	No
Evergreen	Hardy	No
Evergreen	Hardy	Moderate
Evergreen	Hardy	No
Evergreen	Tender	No
Evergreen	Hardy	No
Deciduous	Hardy	No
Evergreen	Moderate	No
Deciduous	Hardy	No
Deciduous	Hardy	No
Evergreen	Hardy	No
Evergreen	Hardy	No
Deciduous	Moderate	Moderate
Evergreen	Hardy	Yes
Deciduous	Hardy	No
Deciduous	Hardy	Yes
Evergreen	Hardy	No
Evergreen	Hardy	Yes
Deciduous	Hardy	Moderate
Deciduous	Hardy	Moderate
Evergreen	Hardy	Yes
Evergreen	Hardy	Yes
Deciduous	Moderate	No
Evergreen	Tender	No
Deciduous	Hardy	No
Deciduous	Hardy	No
Deciduous	Hardy	No
Evergreen	Tender	Moderate
Evergreen	Tender	Moderate
Evergreen	Moderate	No
Deciduous	Hardy	No

[1]Varieties flower at different seasons. Hong Kong is the preferred species with rose-red or purple flowers in winter. They are tender to cold and not salt-tolerant.

[2]Season is variable with species.

Table 3. Common and botanical names of hardy and flowering trees

Apple	*Malus pumila* spp. (three varieties for Florida: Anna, Dorset Golden, Ein Shemex)
Banana shrub	*Michelia fuscata*
Bay, loblolly	*Gordonia lasianthus*
Bay, red	*Persea borbonia*
Bottle brush	*Callistemon citrinus*
Buckeye	*Aesculus*
Camellia	*Camellia japonica*
Camphor	*Cinnamomum camphora*
Candlebush	*Cassia* spp.
Cedar, red	*Juniperus silicicola*
Cherry laurel	*Prunus caroliniana*
Chinaberry	*Melia azedarach*
Chinese tallow	*Sapium sebiferum*
Citrus	*Rutaceae* spp.
Crape myrtle	*Lagerstroemia indica*
Cypress	*Taxodium distichum*
Dogwood	*Cornus florida*
Elm, Chinese	*Ulmus parvifolia*
Elm, Drake	*Ulmus pumila*
Eucalyptus	*Elaeagnus pungens*
Firethorn	*Pyracantha coccinea*
Gardenia	*Gardenia jasminoides*
Golden rain	*Koelreuteria elegans*
Hickory	*Hicoria* spp.
India hawthorn	*Rhaphiolepis indica*
Jacaranda	*Jacaranda mimosifolia*
Jerusalem thorn	*Parkinsonia aculeata*
Ligustrum	*Ligustrum japonicum*
Loquat	*Eriobotrya japonica*
Magnolia	*Magnolia grandiflora*
Maple	*Acer rubrum*
Mimosa	*Albizia julibrissin*
Natal plum	*Carissa grandiflora*
Oak, laurel	*Quercus laurifolia*

Oak, live	*Quercus virginiana*
Oak, water	*Quercus nigra*
Oleander	*Nerium oleander*
Orchid	*Bauhinia purpurea* spp.
Papaya	*Carica papaya* spp.
Peach	*Prunus persica* spp.(sixteen varieties for Florida)
Pear	*Pyrus lecontei* spp. (five varieties for Florida)
Persimmon	*Diospyros kaki* spp. (nine varieties for Florida)
Pine, sand	*Pinus clausa*
Pine, slash	*Pinus caribaea*
Redbud	*Cercis canadensis*
Royal poinciana	*Delonix regia*
Schefflera	*Brassaia actinophylla*
Silk oak	*Grevillea robusta*
Sumac	*Rhus vernix*
Sycamore	*Platanus occidentalis*
Sweet gum	*Liquidambar styraciflua*
Wax myrtle	*Myrica cerifera*
Wild hog plum	*Prunus americana*

Choosing Trees

When choosing trees, first decide what function you wish the tree to serve—the purpose of the tree and the size of the home grounds. Consider what the tree has to offer for each season: foliage color, flowers, fruit, cones, seeds, pods, bark, and interestingly shaped trunks and limbs. Then cross-check the following characteristics with your needs.

Size of trees. What size of tree do you need and where should it be planted? (Refer to tables 1, 2, and 3 for information about each tree.) When choosing trees to be planted near the ocean, be sure to pick those that are drought-, salt-, and wind-tolerant and will thrive in soil lacking in nutriments. The mature height and spread will help determine the type of tree and the placement. It is best to plant far enough from the house to prevent limbs from hanging over the roof.

Tall trees with heavy foliage are subject to excessive storm damage. Gutters filled with fallen leaves can be a constant problem. If you have a small lot, stick to trees of medium or small size. Keep away from power lines if you are considering a tree that will grow tall.

Shade. What kind of shade will be created? Do you want dense shade or bright light under the tree? This will be determined by the type of plants or lawn grass you wish to grow under the tree.

Roots. What kind of root system does the tree of your choice have? Shallow-rooted trees such as citrus, oaks, cypress, eucalyptus, maples, pines, and silk oak wreck the lawn, clog sewers, and break sidewalks and driveways.

Debris. Is your tree clean or does it litter blossoms, leaves, fruit, berries, or peeling bark? Littering trees include bay, camphor, cherry laurel, cypress, golden rain, hickory, magnolia, mimosa, pines, sycamore, and silk oak.

Growth. How fast does the tree grow? Rapidly growing trees are inclined to be brittle, weak, and hazardous. These include bottle brush, camphor, cedar, cherry laurel, eucalyptus, golden rain, and silk oak.

Because of prevailing winds along the coast, many trees need to be staked when they are planted. See the information on staking later in this chapter.

Foliage. Do you want an evergreen tree or one that drops its leaves in the fall (deciduous)? Generally, trees planted to shade the home on the west side should be deciduous in order to let the sunshine in during the winter months. Some of the most popular deciduous trees for residential yards are Chinese tallow, crape myrtle, dogwood, elm, hickory, maple, mimosa, peach, persimmon, redbud, sycamore, and sweetgum.

Number. Do you need one tree or several? The tendency is to overplant without carefully considering mature growth size and spread. If you already have too many trees, study them and eliminate the inferior ones.

❀

When you have taken all of these things into consideration and have decided which tree will fit your needs, get as much information as possible at the time of purchase concerning planting, care, type of soil, sun, shade, diseases, pests, fertilizer, and water requirements. Do keep planting trees. When you run out of room in your own yard for trees, donate some to a school, a church, or a park.

Planting

Planting instructions for trees vary somewhat depending on whether they are purchased with bare roots, balled and burlapped, or in containers. Specific instruction may be obtained from any nursery. In general, however, dig the planting hole wide and deep enough to accommodate the roots plus a mixture of a nutritious soil to be added around the root ball. Put enough good soil at the bottom of the hole so that the top of the root ball will be even with the soil surface—the same depth it grew in the nursery. Keep in mind that water drains rapidly from trees planted in the sandy soil along the ocean and the Gulf Coast. Prevailing winds off the water cause trees to bend away from the wind and keep them sprayed with salt mist. Avoid planting where the water

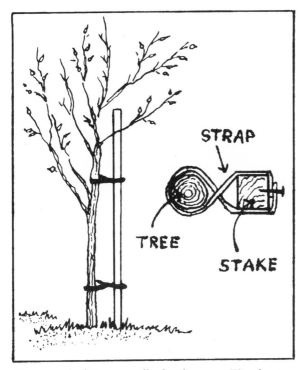

Figure 4. Staking a small, slender tree. Tie the tree to the stake with two or three figure-eight straps, adjusted so that the tree sways slightly.

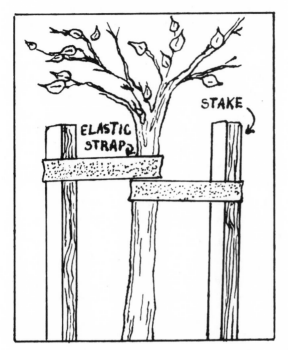

Figure 5. Staking a larger tree. Use two loops of elastic webbing, which allow for flexibility of movement while holding the trunk upright.

table is so high that the soil cannot remain aerated. Try to choose trees that will thrive in your type of soil, or find out whether your soil can be amended to meet the needs of the particular species you have chosen. Most trees seem to grow best in a soil that is slightly acid (pH 6 to 7).

Staking

In order to give them a good start, some trees need to be staked. It is important that this be done correctly.

Staking does three things: anchors, supports, and protects. The root ball needs to be anchored until it has had time to grow new roots and establish good support. Stakes help to form a straight, upright tree and can also protect the trunk from damage by equipment—lawn mowers, string trimmers, and vandals.

Staking is especially important near the seacoast, where consistent prevailing winds promote leaning; where the soil is loose, porous sand;

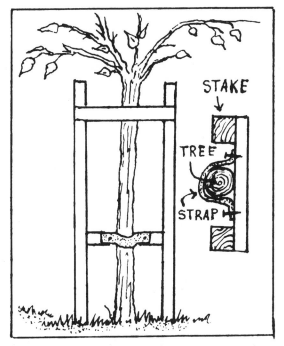

Figure 6. Staking a tree taller than ten feet. Use two stakes to brace trees. Alternate crosspieces for better support.

and where the water table is usually high. Water and wind cause sinking and shifting before the tree has had time to get a firm grip in the surrounding earth. Soil can then filter in around the trunk of the tree and bury it too deep. Many kinds of shrubs and trees in this condition will not grow properly.

Staking should be done when the tree is planted. Drive supporting stakes next to the root ball. Fill up the hole with more good soil, tamping it firmly around the trunk. Ridge the soil to form a saucer around the trunk. Attach the plant to supporting stakes with proper tie material, water well, and watch it grow.

If you purchase a plant in a container and find that the trunk is leaning, you may tip the root ball over a bit in the hole at planting time so that the trunk is upright. Stakes will hold the position until the trunk rights itself.

The type of stake is determined by the size of the shrub or tree. Use inconspicuous stakes and ties when possible. Stakes can be metal

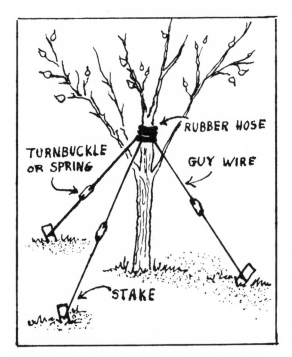

Figure 7. Staking a specimen lawn tree. Guy
wires, run through pieces of garden hose and
anchored to stakes, are good support.

or treated wood and may be painted green for disguise. Metal stakes
should have a flange just below the ground surface for extra stability.
Bamboo holds up well for staking smaller plants. Stakes should have
as small a caliber as possible so that they won't shade the trunks.

Make the stakes as short as possible but tall enough to hold the
plant upright under calm conditions. Top support for plants should
be as low on the trunk as possible but high enough so that the tree
will return to its upright position after deflection by the wind. To find
the proper height, hold the trunk in one hand, pull the top to one
side, and release. Repeat at various levels. The height at which the
trunk will return to upright when the top is released is the height at
which to attach the ties. This point should be near the top of the stakes.
Ties should be flexible but not enough to allow the tree to contact
the stakes. Make sure that the tree won't be injured by rubbing or
girdling.

Several materials are available for tying plants to anchor or support stakes. No matter what you use, the tie material should contact the tree with a broad surface and have flexibility to minimize rubbing or girdling. Elastic webbing, old tire cording, inner tubes cut into circles to form strips, wire slipped inside pieces of garden hose, and nylon stockings are some suggestions for ties. There are several materials that you can purchase especially for this purpose.

Small, slender plants. Trees that will not have to be staked for a long period of time can be braced with only one slender stake a few inches away from the trunk. Sink the stake into the ground about one foot deep and tie the trunk to the stake with two or three figure-eight straps, adjusted so that the tree can sway slightly. This type of stake should not be left in place too long because it has been found that the shadow on the trunk behind the stake and the root system in the area do not develop properly.

Larger trees. For larger trees, a single tie between two stakes, looped around the trunk halfway between the stakes, may be all you need. The tie should be fairly loose around the trunk, tied so that the loop around the trunk can't work toward a support stake in a strong wind. Sink the stake into the ground about one foot deep and tie the stake with two or three figure-eight straps, adjusted so that the three can sway slightly. However, in windy areas, a loop around each stake can minimize injury.

Trees taller than ten feet. These trees need two or three stakes tall enough to support the particular tree and need to be driven at least eighteen inches into the ground. The line drawn between the two stakes should be at right angles to the most troublesome wind direction. Place the cross-tie to the lee of the stakes to cut down on possible rubbing.

Very large trees. These trees may require guy wires. This is usually done by fastening three wires around the trunk inside rubber hoses to protect the bark where they join the tree. The wires are anchored to the ground with weights or stakes. Springs or turnbuckles can be purchased to attach to the wires, allowing for flexibility and tightening when necessary.

❀

CHAPTER 4

Landscaping

Balconies

Balconies have been transformed into backyards for thousands of apartment, condominium, and townhouse dwellers across the country. Many types of gardens can be created on balconies for both their beauty and their benefits. A balcony garden can offer splashes of color, herbs for seasoning, flowering fruit trees, container-grown vegetables—almost anything except a lawn.

Just remember, when planning your balcony garden, choose the right plant for the correct location, learning its needs and growth habits and whether or not it is hardy to cold, wind, and salt spray.

This type of garden can open up a whole new world for you. Try it, but start with a few choice plants and enlarge as you become more experienced. Do be careful to choose the right plant for the correct exposure.

Sun and Wind

Planning must start with sun and wind exposure because these will be the most difficult elements to control. Your selection of plants will depend upon the direction that your balcony faces. Plant choices for north, south, east, or west will be quite different from one another.

Spring is the ideal time to plant a balcony garden, but you can have something growing out there throughout the entire year. Just remember that July, August, and September are the hottest months on the coast. March, early April, and the fall months are the windiest times.

Safety Precautions

Safety precautions come next. Find out just how much weight your balcony can handle. And for goodness' sake, keep in mind that the balcony below you might not belong to a gardener. Think ahead about dripping water and sifting sand.

Containers

Select a container of the right size and shape for the growth characteristics and appearance of your plant. A handsome plant deserves a handsome planter.

All containers should have drainage holes in the bottom. If not, put a one-inch layer of pebbles or other coarse material underneath the soil in the pot, and be extra careful not to overwater. The use of a water meter can take the guesswork out of this important part of container gardening. Meters can be bought at garden supply stores.

Plants need room enough for good growth. It is better to have the pots a little too large rather than a little too small. When repotting, choose a pot one to three inches wider than the old one. Fiber or plastic pots are not as heavy to handle as clay ones. However, clay and wooden ones breathe and offer better drainage than plastic pots do. If your balcony is large enough for a half-barrel, it makes an attractive container for larger plants or mini-gardens.

Various sizes of wooden boxes are also attractive containers. They should be made of durable lumber such as cypress, redwood, heart of pine, or cedar, and be painted with a preservative (not creosote). The ends of the boards should be sealed. In general, a convenient size for a box is three by four feet and at least six inches deep, but take into consideration the space available on the balcony. The boxes should be elevated on supports for good drainage. To prevent the possibility of leaking onto lower balconies, place drip pans under the boxes.

Soil

Use a porous, fast-draining soil mix. Commercial mixes are best because they are light and sterile and don't harbor insects, diseases, and weeds. When filling your container with soil, leave at least two inches between the soil surface and the top of the container to accommodate water.

Mulches on top of the soil will help hold moisture and regulate soil temperature. Good mulches to use are shredded bark, wood chips, wood nuggets, sphagnum moss, pine needles, and oak leaves.

Choice of Plants

Pick the right plant for the right spot. Choose those that have compact growth and thrive in limited space. There are many dwarf varieties available. Be sure that the eventual height and width fit your garden space and that the plant meets the necessary climatic conditions (wind, sun, heat, cold). Climbing plants will need a trellis, and cascading plants will need hanging baskets or window boxes.

It is best to buy plantlets and transplant them in your containers. Water the young plants well and protect them from direct sun for the first few days. Thin plantlets while they are small. Discard the weak and leave the strong ones, but don't leave so many that your container seems crowded.

However, it's pleasant to start from seeds with some of the quick-sprouting flowers, herbs, and vegetables (such as peas, beans, radishes, lettuce, Swiss chard, squash, nasturtium, marigold, dianthus, gaillardia, impatiens, calendula, cosmos, zinnia, stock, and ageratum) and watch them pop up and develop.

If your balcony isn't any higher than three stories, be sure to include some plants that will attract butterflies. Butterflies are usually attracted to simple flowers and bright colors. Some hardy, salt-tolerant plants with flowers that will supply nectar and will thrive in containers are African daisy, alyssum, bush daisy, butterfly weed, coreopsis, dianthus, dusty miller, gaillardia, gazania daisy, goldenrod, kalanchoe, lantana, marguerite, partridge pea, periwinkle, portulaca, prickly pear cactus, sea lavender, sea marigold, verbena, and zinnia.

Other things that can be grown from seeds sown directly in pots or window boxes are parsley, spring onions, spinach, kale, garlic, carrots, and cucumbers. However, these will need some protection from wind and salt spray. If you want a continuous harvest, sow seeds at weekly intervals.

Water and Fertilizer

Balcony plants require lots of water but must have good drainage. They should be kept evenly moist but not soggy wet. In a very hot spot, it helps to insert the pot into another container slightly larger and pack the space in between with damp sphagnum moss or vermiculite.

Flowers that don't require a lot of water are lantana, marigolds, salvia, vinca, kalanchoe, aloe, gaillardia, periwinkle, and gazania daisy.

Container plants have big appetites because frequent watering washes nutrients out of the growing medium. Feed them regularly with a complete, balanced fertilizer that dissolves in water. I like to put a weak solution of fertilizer in the water every time I water. Follow directions on the fertilizer package. It's easier to keep tabs on the water and fertilizer schedule if you have a specific day of the week for this chore.

Exposures

Nearly all vegetables must have at least six hours of sunshine a day. Sometimes it's necessary to move containers around a bit in order to meet this need.

Plants that do well in the shadier areas of a northern exposure include impatiens, looseleaf lettuce, cast-iron plant (*Aspidistra elatior*), ferns, Swedish ivy, English ivy, lady palm (*Raphis excelsa*), areca palm, fan palm, sentry palm, spider plant, rubber tree, Norfolk Island pine (*Araucaria excelsa*), philodendron, dieffenbachia, schefflera, stock, dianthus, begonia, and periwinkle. The palms are not salt-resistant on the oceanfront. Root crops and leaf vegetables can grow with less sunshine than other types of vegetables.

Southern or eastern exposures are the most desirable for growing the majority of plants, such as cucumbers, squash, melons, beans, peas, tomatoes, gardenias, azaleas, crape myrtle, roses, and most flowers.

Tomatoes, squash, and cucumbers may need to be staked. Using twist ties, gently secure vines such as bougainvillea, Confederate jasmine, man-devilla, allamanda, and morning glory to a trellis.

Dwarf cucumbers, peas, and many herbs, including chives, basil, marjoram, thyme, mint, parsley, and sage, can be grown in hanging baskets and brought indoors when the weather turns cold. Smaller varieties of tomatoes—Cherry, Pixie, and Patio—do well in hanging baskets.

Cacti, succulents, sansevieria, portulaca, gaillardia, and periwinkle are about the only plants that will tolerate full western sun and the heat reflected from the walls of a building.

Pests

Unfortunately, having your garden high above the earth doesn't eliminate pests. Keep a close watch and spray as necessary. Don't spray on a windy day.

VEGETABLE GARDENS

Gardening has become one of the most popular hobbies because it is suitable for everyone. Whether you're a senior citizen, a youngster, or any age between, you can enjoy growing things. And regardless of the size of your garden—large, small, or just some pots—it's fun to grow a few vegetables, herbs, and pretty flowers. If you want to try gardening but don't know where to start, just follow this outline of basic gardening practices.

Planning

Garden plan. Start with a plan on paper. Draw a layout showing rows, spaces, and varieties of vegetables, fruits, and flowers you wish to grow. Decide what you want to plant, and how much. This should be based on the vegetables your family enjoys and the amount you can use. If you are a new gardener, start with a few basic vegetables such as carrots, radishes, onions, and lettuce. Don't allow your garden to become a burden by over-planting. You can add plants when you have become more experienced. Get to know your vegetables—plant cool-weather crops in fall, spring crops in March, and warm-weather crops in late spring. See the calendars in chapter 5 for what to plant and when.

Garden location. Plan your backyard garden so that it will blend with your landscaping. It should be conveniently located, readily accessible to water and garden supplies, and protected from wind.

Most vegetables need full sun; but some tender ones, such as lettuces, do better in partial shade from a tree, a fence, or a row of corn.

Select and mark off your garden site. Choose a spot away from the roots of trees and shrubs; free from low, moist places; and with at least six hours of sun each day. An easy plan is to measure your site carefully, drive stakes at the four corners, and run a string around the perimeter. This will help determine the number of rows in the available space and help keep the rows straight.

Vegetables such as carrots, lettuces, radishes, cabbages, and kale can be used as borders in a flower bed.

Soil Preparation

Readying the soil. Ideally, planting sites should be prepared several days or weeks before planting. Start by removing all vegetation in the garden area. Thoroughly spade the soil to a depth of six to eight inches. If your garden is rather large, buy or rent a rotary tilling machine that will do most of the soil clearing and tilling in one process.

Break up all the clumps and cultivate until your soil is fine and crumbly. Then rake well with an iron-toothed rake to remove stones and other debris. For sandy soil, work in several inches of compost, peat, manures, or other organic materials to improve soil condition. Try to estimate a soil consistency of about one-third sand, one-third compost, and one-third peat. If it doesn't seem to drain well, add more compost and sand. Peat absorbs water. Sand and compost aid drainage.

Nutrition. After the soil is well tilled, and before it is raked smooth, apply a balanced fertilizer, preferably organic. Wettable sulfur or an acid-forming fertilizer, such as ammonium sulfate or camellia/azalea mix, can be used to help lower the pH when your soil is too alkaline. Apply according to the directions on the package. It's a good idea to have the pH of your soil tested. Most vegetables do well with a slightly acid pH (6 to 7). See the section on soil in chapter 1.

Level and smooth the surface with a rake unless you are planning to plant some things in hills and furrows, perhaps potatoes, vine crops, strawberries, or melons.

To prepare hills (raised beds), rake enriched soil into hills about a foot higher than trenches between the hills. Each year fill the trenches with organic materials (compost, manures). This compost will soak up and store excessive moisture, slowly releasing it to the plants growing on the hills. At the end of the season, take the soil from each hill and throw it on top of the organic waste in the furrows, thus creating a new set of hills and valleys. After years of gardening in this way, you will have very rich soil.

Planting

Seeds. A *seed bed* is the place you have prepared for planting your seeds. Seed beds can be trays, boxes, a cold frame, or any protected area. The seed bed is a nursery for producing seedlings to be transplanted. Some seeds can be planted directly in the garden. You will need to learn which vegetables require the nursery treatment and which ones do not (see chapter 5, August and September calendars). Those planted directly in the garden usually have to be thinned after they develop at least two healthy leaves.

Some gardeners prepare a tiny trench in which to drop their seeds by drawing a line with a stick or pressing a narrow board down the center of the row. A general rule is to cover seeds with soil, which has been broken down into fine particles, to a depth equal to three times the diameter of the seeds. Sprinkling lightly with the hose will settle the seeds sufficiently. Do not press them down.

Sow seeds according to instructions on the seed packet. Seed packets from reliable seed companies give detailed information on when, where, and how to plant each species. Also, check the expiration date on the packet to be sure you are not buying old seeds.

It isn't possible to recommend exact planting dates for Florida gardeners because weather patterns vary greatly from year to year. We may have a winter with as many as four hard freezes, or we may experience a warm winter with little or no frost. The same is true of rainfall. Our wet and dry seasons used to be rather clearly defined, but we can no longer depend on consistency. Therefore, the precise time to plant is a decision that must be made by the gardener, depending upon the seasonal weather and where your garden is located in the state.

The average dooryard gardener plants two gardens a year—March/April/May and September/October. More experienced gardeners can have four gardens a year, and some gardeners plant something every month of the year. Northern Florida gardeners generally plant a few weeks later than those in central Florida, and southern Florida gardeners plant a few weeks earlier than the dates indicated in the calendars in chapter 5.

The placement of each species requires careful planning. Most vegetables require full sun, but some need semishade. Plant or transplant tall growers, such as sweet corn, pole beans, staked tomatoes, and tall sunflowers, on the north side of a garden so they won't shade shorter varieties that need full sun. Most vine crops have similar requirements for good growth and are subject to the same insect and disease problems. Therefore, if they are planted in the same general area, maintenance will be easier.

Tending

Growing space. Properly space plants so they will receive enough air, nutrients, sunlight, and moisture. Thin seedlings or transplant according to the space recommended on seed packets. Remove the weak and leave or transplant the strong. Crowded plants will be weak and spindly and will produce and flower poorly. Gently cultivate the soil around the seedlings until they are large enough for you to apply a good mulch. Mulch will help hold moisture and discourage weed growth. Weeds that come through can be pulled by hand.

Moisture. Water your garden site well and let the water soak in before planting. Prewatering settles the soil and provides a reservoir of moisture that will be pulled upward through the soil by capillary action.

Fertilizer. The most important rule regarding fertilizing is to apply the right kind, in the right amounts, at the right times. Don't overfertilize. Your nursery supplier will be glad to help you with this. See the section on fertilizer in chapter 1.

Insect and disease control. Select healthy plants and disease-resistant varieties. Rotate crops from year to year, remove plants that appear sick and dispose of them in plastic bags, and keep your plants healthy so they will have natural resistance to disease and environmental conditions.

There are only a few major insects, diseases, fungi, and scales that invade gardens, and it isn't difficult to recognize them. All of these conditions can be eradicated if the treatment is started soon enough. Learn what to watch for and act quickly.

Some garden sites need to have the soil fumigated to eliminate nematodes, weeds, soil-borne insects, and diseases. The usual routine is to garden once and, if you have followed these instructions and still have poor results, have your soil tested and then fumigate if necessary.

Companion planting is a good idea to add beauty and to discourage insect attacks. Herbs such as dill, fennel, onion, chive, leek, parsley, basil, sage, and tarragon are said to be beneficial as insect repellents. The pungent odor of marigolds and nasturtiums is another deterrent.

Harvest

Pick and use fruits and vegetables at their peak of flavor and goodness. Don't allow overmaturity, especially with zucchini, cucumbers, and broccoli. Corn is sweetest if picked early in the morning. Store peas and corn in the refrigerator immediately after picking unless they are cooked promptly. Beet greens should be cut at least one inch from the top of the beet. Share with friends, freeze, can, or otherwise store surplus produce for future meals.

Extending Your Harvest Season

Continuous plantings every few weeks will extend your harvest. Basically there are two types of succession plantings: multiple plantings of the same crop and those that follow different crops recommended for the next season. A summer crop of bush beans, okra, eggplant, and loosehead lettuce can be planted in a place vacated by early, fast-maturing vegetables such as radishes and Bibb lettuce. Replace spring onions with leeks, spring tomatoes with warm-weather peas and okra, and bell peppers with spinach. Radish, snap beans, lettuce, and sweet corn can be planted about every two weeks for a long harvesting period. Spinach, collards, turnips, and cabbage planted in the spring will thrive almost all summer. Rotate the crop planting sites to avoid depleting the soil of certain nutrients and to discourage pests attracted to specific plants. Legumes will add nitrogen to the soil.

All of this know-how should keep your garden space, and you, busy producing tasty vegetables year round.

ORGANIC GARDENING

The purpose of this section is not to give instructions on how to garden organically but to help you understand the concept. Organic gardening requires special skills and wisdom that comes with a great deal of practice. Organic gardeners know the value of careful observation of their plants, whether that entails signs of a lack of proper nutrition or the invasion of insects. They know intrinsic things, such as the fact that leaf crops remove nitrogen from the soil and legumes replace it. They know that if you rotate your crops yearly, you will decrease insect infestation and the buildup of soil diseases.

Perhaps inorganic products are easier to obtain and to apply, but organic materials release their nutrients slowly and over a longer period of time. Plants fed inorganic fertilizers often develop signs of deficiencies that rarely occur when plants are fed organically. Also, organic produce is generally thought to be better for your health, more nutritious, and better tasting than that from inorganic gardens. Learning to become an organic gardener may take several years, so start

small and don't be discouraged. Just keep in mind that success starts
with healthy soil.

Organic versus Inorganic

What is the difference between the terms *inorganic* and *organic?* Inorganic refers to chemical compounds or substances composed of matter that is not animal or vegetable and is intended for use as soil amendments or for pest and disease control. These substances are usually
man-made rather than arising from natural growth. They include commercial insecticides, pesticides, and fungicides and are available in the
form of liquids, dusts, and granules.

In order to simplify the concept of organic gardening, recall the
methods used by the American Indians and the early settlers of this
country. Basic organic gardening was their standard procedure. It's
not like that anymore, for many reasons that we will discuss in the
following paragraphs.

In general, organic gardeners don't use commercial fertilizers or
chemical pesticides and insecticides. They depend on organics such
as compost, animal manures, peat, cover crops (green manure), interplanting, companion planting, crop rotation, and natural controls for
pests—plus knowledge of the requirements of each species, including
fertilizer, sunshine, and water.

Many gardeners today are attempting to return to true organic
methods, but an awful lot of others are forced to combine organic
and modern scientific discoveries (inorganic products). Why? There
are several reasons. (1) We have so many more insects and diseases
with which to cope, (2) our soils have been depleted of many of their
nutrients, (3) in many areas salt has intruded into the groundwater,
and (4) a lot of us don't have time to go out and catch fish to bury
under our plants.

Tips for Organic Gardening

Selecting vegetables. When planting their gardens, organic gardeners select vegetables that are less damaged by insects and diseases and

that can be more successfully grown without the use of pesticides. These include (but are not limited to) beets, carrots, Swiss chard, collards, sweet potatoes, turnips, onions, radishes, and parsnips. Also, in order to avoid problems caused by rain and wind, hot summer weather, and possible freezes, they plant according to the best time to harvest.

Making compost. Organic gardens begin with a good compost pile. At least one compost pile is a must. If you have the space, have several in various stages of decomposition. (See the section on compost in chapter 1.) When material from plant and animal origin breaks down in the compost pile, we refer to it as peat, humus, or loam—rich, healthy, organic soil. This material contains carbon compounds needed to maintain healthy soil structure and microbacterial life. A compost pile needs earthworms to keep the soil loose so there's space for oxygen aeration and better drainage. Earthworms also enrich the soil by continually eating and excreting.

Organic Controls for Pests and Diseases

The warm, humid climate of the South promotes extensive insect and disease problems that are much worse in the summer months. However, organic gardeners expect and tolerate some insect damage—for example, on the outer leaves of cabbage, which can be easily removed at harvest.

Specific controls. Organic gardeners know their insects and how to use natural controls—when to use them and which plants will tolerate them. They know to use the nicotine in tobacco for aphids and thrips; oil sprays for scales, sucking insects, insect eggs, and mites; copper for fungi; insecticide soaps and oils for aphids and ants; sulfur for bacteria and fungi; nontoxic sticky flypaper for all flying insects; wood ashes for maggots; and boric acid, red pepper, and garlic juice for almost all insects.

Bacillus thuringiensis is a biological spray that infects the insides of caterpillars, causing illness severe enough to kill. Pyrethrum powder, a nerve poison made from plant material, is used against flies, leafhoppers, and cabbage worms. Rotenone, a poison extracted from roots, is used to kill beetles and corn borers.

However, pyrethrum and rotenone will also kill beneficial insects. Therefore, keep in mind that all of these products can be harmful to humans if used carelessly and improperly.

Beneficial insects. Insects such as praying mantis, ladybugs and ladybug larvae, lacewings, dragonflies, and certain varieties of mites and wasps are called "good" insects. Unfortunately, chemical materials have helped destroy many of them.

Toads eat cutworms and other small insects. Some birds eat an amazing number of insects each day. Put out a bird feeder and a bird bath to encourage birds to come to your yard. Beneficial insects are drawn to flowers for nectar and pollen, so every garden should have blooming plants at all times. White sweet alyssum, sunflowers, Queen Anne's lace, daisies, clover, and flowering herbs are some suggestions. Organic gardeners allow some vegetables to go to seed in order to have flowers for beneficial insects. Also, they allow some flowering weeds to live in their gardens.

Companion planting. The theory of companion planting is controversial. Nevertheless, some organic gardeners believe that corn planted with velvet beans or peas allows the beans or peas to give nitrogen to the corn's roots, while the cornstalks provide climbing poles for these vines. Corn can be planted to cast shade on tender vegetables such as lettuce, melons, squash, and cucumbers. Onions, chives, and garlic will help discourage insects. However, onions inhibit the growth of peas and beans. French marigolds are supposed to suppress rootknot. The cabbage family—cabbage, cauliflower, broccoli, Brussels sprout, kohlrabi—is beneficial to potatoes when plowed under and used as green manure. Radishes planted near vine crops will keep beetles away. Nasturtiums repel squash bugs. Many herbs possess aromatic fragrances that may serve as repellents.

Organic Fertilizers

Suggestions for organic fertilizers include compost; blood meal and cottonseed meal for high nitrogen; bone meal for calcium and phosphorus; fish emulsion for nitrogen, phosphorus, and potash; wood ashes for potash; and aged manure for complete nutrients. Manures must not be too old, or many elements will be leached out. Moreover, they should not be fresh because fresh manure can burn plants. Compost fresh manures for several weeks. Kelp meal, made from seaweed, contains many of the nutrients needed by plants.

Establishing a New Lawn

A nice lawn is a challenge. However, if you take the time to learn what it's all about, you can avoid many of the frustrations and enjoy the luxury of having a beautiful new or reestablished lawn.

Planning

Springtime is ideal for starting a new lawn, but it can be done successfully year round. Hot and cold months have their drawbacks and less chance for success.

The first thing you need to do is study your site and decide what kind of grasses will thrive there. One variety will probably not do well in all areas of your yard. See the section on lawn grasses for hot, humid climates later in this chapter.

Soil and Sustenance

Soil preparation. Soil preparation and renovation are the next steps. Rake the areas vigorously, removing all debris—old grass, weeds, sticks, stones, and roots. Loosen the soil several inches deep by using a hoe or heavy rake. It is even better to cultivate the soil to a depth of about six inches with a rototiller. This tool can be rented.

When possible, avoid planting seeds or laying sod on plain sand. Try to improve existing soil with some kind of organic material. You don't need to use pure black dirt (peat). A combination of peat, clean red dirt, clean topsoil, and seasoned manures well blended with your sandy soil will give your lawn a fertile foundation in which to grow. This layer should be about three inches deep.

The soil mixture I have suggested will contain nutrients and will hold moisture long enough for roots to benefit. Lawn soil pH should be slightly acid (6.5 to 7). If you are laying a sod lawn, save enough soil mixture to fill the spaces between pads after the sod is laid. Water it to smooth the surface. When ordering red dirt, be sure it's from a deep pit free of roots and weed seeds.

Rake the soil smooth, paying attention to possible drainage problems in different areas of your yard. The entire lawn area must drain properly. Fill in low spots, and smooth out humps and bumps before laying the sod. Lawns should slope away from the house. If you are going to seed or sprig your new lawn, the surface should be slightly higher than any existing lawn, because the soil will settle. If you are going to lay new sod, allow for the thickness of the sod when determining your finished lawn height.

Nurturing the new lawn. When planting seeds, follow the instructions on the package very carefully. Seeded areas should be kept uniformly moist at all times while the seed is germinating and until the grass is at least two inches high. Water with a light spray to avoid washing away seeds. To discourage birds from eating your seeds, place wind whirly-birds around the area. Don't mow until new grass passes the two-inch mark. After the grass is growing well, raise the mower blades to three inches.

Tending

Fertilizing. Fertilizer requirements differ with the species of grass. You must learn what is needed for the type you have chosen. A new sod lawn should be fertilized lightly with a complete balanced product about a month after it starts to grow. An established St. Augustine lawn should require only two applications of fertilizer a year—spring and fall. Shady areas can benefit by the addition of an acid-producing fertilizer, such as camellia/azalea, organic, or wettable sulfur. Fertilizers can be applied as liquid sprays or pellets. Slow-release pellets last longer than other fertilizers. It is best to apply fertilizer to a wet lawn. Water, fertilize, and then water again. Too much fertilizer, or fertilizer left on the grass blades, can burn blades and roots.

Watering. Proper watering is especially important. Fungus and diseases are likely to develop in areas that don't receive a lot of sun and are kept constantly damp. Shallow, sporadic watering encourages weak surface roots that parch and die in summer heat. Adjust your watering schedule to the seasons and the amount of rainfall. Never water unless needed. Don't allow the reach of sprinklers to overlap. It is best to water well to a depth of several inches each time instead of sprinkling lightly and more frequently. Deep watering encourages the roots to grow down, which helps you avoid a spongy lawn and surface roots that can be burned by the sun.

Weeding. Weeds are common to all lawn grasses. They compete for water, nutrients, and sunlight. However, a few weeds will do no harm, and a vigorously growing lawn will usually smother most of them. Creeping Charlie, dollarweed, beggarweed, clover, and crabgrass are five exceptions. Dig them out or use a herbicide at their onset before they destroy your lawn. Both preemergence and postemergence herbicides are sometimes necessary for a good weed control program. Keep in mind that using the incorrect herbicide on your lawn can seriously damage it.

Insect Control

Kinds of insects. The six main insects that invade lawns are grubs, armyworms, chinch bugs, sod webworms, mole crickets, and lawn leafhoppers.

Grubs are the larvae of beetles. They look something like a plump, white embryo and are found in the soil quietly feeding on the roots of grasses and plants. They can destroy a lawn by themselves or with the help of armadillos and ground moles, who come to dig for the grubs. A sign of grub damage is when the lawn looks as if it needs to be watered and you know that it doesn't. There are several specific insecticides available for controlling grubs.

Armyworms are hatched from night-flying moths. They average about one and one-half inches long and are easy to see in areas where leaf blades have been skeletonized. They can be eradicated with a recommended spray.

Chinch bugs can appear from April to October because they prefer hot, dry weather. They suck the sap from grass blades and usually work in a circle. Examine the roots of green grass around the brown areas for live bugs. These pests are not easy to see because they have several stages of development—orange, red, and brown. They travel at a rapid rate of speed, so you have to look quickly when trying to identify them.

Sod webworms are a terrible lawn enemy. Webworm moths arrive in early summer and drop their eggs over grassy areas. The eggs hatch in about seven days. The short caterpillars feed at night near the soil surface and skeletonize blades of grass. Older ones cut the blades off completely and form tunnels of silk and grass, feeding within the tunnels. They leave behind a sodden, thick bunch of gunk. The result is irregular brown patches of dead grass. The webs are easy to spot in the early morning while the dew is still on the grass.

Mole crickets are insects with shovel-like feet for making tunnels in the soil that disturb and cut off grass roots. Adults place eggs in underground cells. Eggs hatch in warm weather and become adults. They leave brown streaks and wilted grass that will pull up easily. Mole crickets are found more commonly in soft, newly planted areas and can be a serious problem in established turf.

Lawn leafhoppers make themselves known when you mow. If there is a severe infestation, cricket-like bugs will jump rapidly out of the grass in all directions. Adults lay eggs in plant tissue. Both adults and nymphs suck juice from the stems and undersides of leaves. While feeding, they inject a toxic saliva that distorts and stunts plant growth and causes tip burn and yellowed, curled leaves. They are difficult to eradicate.

Pest control. Lawn insects are a nuisance and become a bigger problem in warm weather. The secret to success is to identify them at the very first onset and spray the small areas with an insecticide. Always get professional advice about the correct product for eradication.

Lawn Grasses for Hot, Humid Climates

There are only a few varieties of lawn grasses that will tolerate conditions along coastlines in warm climates. It's very important that you choose the right type for your particular purposes. That choice is governed by a number of things.

Characteristics of Grasses That Thrive in Heat and Humidity

Individual grass species have special preferences about fertilizer; soil acidity or alkalinity; sun or shade; dry or wet ground; resistance to certain diseases and pests; abuse from heavy traffic; and tolerance to salt, wind, and drought. Sometimes a single strain of grass is used exclusively, but often lawns are a combination of several kinds. Mixtures offer many advantages.

No single type of grass is likely to suit every part of a lawn. Sun- and shade-tolerant grasses can be used depending upon the demands of your garden. Several types can be combined when each has some desirable characteristic that is lacking in others. There are creeping grasses and bunchlike grasses. Creeping grasses require more frequent mowing and edging but grow into bare spots more readily.

Most warm-climate grasses spread by sending out lateral stems from which new plants take root and grow at intervals. Bits, or clumps, of these stems are called rhizomes if they grow below the ground or stolons if they creep along the surface. They can be placed in the ground to spread and grow together, forming a lawn. Lawns started by this method take longer to establish but are generally healthier and firmer than a lawn that has been completely sodded.

There are several St. Augustine (*Stenotaphrum secundatum*) varieties, but Bitter Blue, Floratine, Floratam, and Pursley's Seville are the most widely used along the coast. All three have good and bad points. They are all fast-growing and have good tolerance for weed control, herbicides, salt spray, hot sun, and some drought. Their medium-width blades have good color. St. Augustine grasses will thrive in a variety of soils if fertilized and watered properly but grow best in soil that is slightly acid. There are no seeds for St. Augustine grasses. They have to be sodded in pads, plugged, or sprigged.

Varieties of Grass for Seacoast Lawns

St. Augustine Bitter Blue. This is the most popular lawn grass for warm climates. The runners are close together, and each joint is capable of putting down roots, producing a lush lawn quite rapidly. Bitter Blue will tolerate salt, hot sun, semishade, and some low temperatures. A freeze can cause browning, but warm weather and water will bring back the green growth.

Pursley's Seville. This is a hybrid St. Augustine grass that has excellent salt-tolerance, thrives in shade if there is good light, and is more resistant to diseases and insects than Bitter Blue. It has a slightly wider leaf blade and a shorter leaf length. This type is excellent for spot repair in an old lawn.

Floratine and Floratam. These are improved varieties of Bitter Blue. They can be mowed shorter, have shown some resistance to chinch bugs and disease, but do not tolerate much shade.

Centipede (*Eremochloa ophiuroides*). This grass is sometimes called "poor man's grass" because it gets by on little food and moisture, providing a low-maintenance lawn. It can be grown from seeds, pads, or sprigs. Centipede has runners, is fine in texture, grows slower and closer to the ground than other grasses, and is more resistant to diseases and insects. It is especially satisfactory for sloping lawns. Centipede doesn't have to be mowed as often as most other lawn grasses.

Centipede requires full sun and is only slightly salt-resistant. Too much fertilizer will turn it yellow, but color can be restored with an application of iron.

Spring is the best time to sow Centipede seeds because they won't germinate unless the ground is quite warm. The soil must be kept moist throughout germination, which takes six weeks or longer. Sow seeds a little heavier than package directions indicate because birds and insects demand a fair share.

Argentine Bahia (*Paspalum notatum*). This is a coarse grass that has been developed for lawn use from the commercial Pensacola pasture grass. It isn't quite as coarse as Pensacola Bahia, seeds less, and doesn't grow as tall. It is recommended for problem areas where the soil is poor and dry.

Argentine Bahia is used along the shoulders of highways and sometimes in pastures. The coarse texture of the blades isn't as pleasant to walk on, and the appearance isn't as nice as the other lawn grasses, but it is resistant to drought, insects, fungus, and heavy traffic. However, it does not do well too close to the ocean or the Gulf because it has no tolerance for salt spray and no runners to encourage spreading. Seed is readily available.

Bermuda (*Cynodon dactylon*). Lawns seeded or sprigged with Bermuda grass are very hardy. This grass is a vigorous grower with such deep roots that it can become a nuisance by invading areas where it isn't wanted. It has fair salt and drought tolerance. Bermuda isn't killed by frost but will turn brown until new spring growth appears.

Zoysia (*Zoisia* spp.). This grass is classified as a warm-climate grass. It makes a lovely lawn but falls into the high-maintenance class in Florida. Some varieties will survive severe winter weather but will turn brown after a freeze. Their texture is very fine and forms a dense turf, which makes them popular for putting greens. Zoysias are slow growers but are salt-tolerant, adapt to a wide range of soils, and are somewhat shade- and drought-tolerant. They will not tolerate damp soil or overwatering and are subject to the usual pest problems. Zoysia grass propagates by seed, sod, sprigs, or plugs.

Italian rye (*Lolium multiflorum*). Sometimes called Oregon rye, this is an excellent grass for warm climates in the cooler months. It adapts well, thrives in sun or shade, and tolerates mowing. Sow in the fall after permanent lawn grass has reached its dormancy (October to December). Broadcast across the existing lawn in an even manner in order to avoid a patchy appearance when the cold weather arrives and turns other grasses brown. These grasses are quick to germinate and have aggressive root systems. Ryes are annuals that die out in late spring about the time that permanent lawn grass starts to grow. Seeds must be kept moist after sown to ensure proper germination.

Dichondra (*D. micrantha*). This isn't a grass but a delightful ground cover used for lawns. Dichondra has lovely, round, cup-shaped leaves that create a smooth, even turf. It will grow in the shade and in other places where lawn grasses don't survive. Dichondra stays green for the entire year except in extremely cold weather. If frozen, it will come back in the spring.

Dichondra spreads rapidly by shallow, rather fragile runners and is excellent for filling in bare spots. Mowing is rarely necessary. It combines with other grasses nicely for an overall green appearance. Seeds are available.

Sometimes dichondra is confused with dollarweed and eradicated. This is unfortunate. Dollarweed has a much larger, thicker leaf and strong runners and will destroy a lawn if allowed to spread. Although the green of a lawn is usually grass, don't overlook the possibilities that other groundcovers can offer. Groundcovers can be used as a grass substitute or as companions for grass. See the section on groundcovers later in this chapter.

Choose your lawn grass according to the demands of your environment, such as soil pH, sun, shade, dry, wet, abuse from traffic and salt, wind, and drought tolerance.

Helping Your Lawn Recover

A beautiful lawn is a luxury, but there are many reasons that explain why we value them. They help beautify the neighborhood; purify and cool the air; provide a place of beauty and relaxation for family, employees, or visitors; reflect positively on the owner; increase real estate value; provide a comfortable place to entertain, work, or visit; and provide a safe, high-quality play area for children.

Florida summers are often hot and dry and winters cold and dry. Rainfall is erratic—too much or not enough. These conditions can have an adverse effect on lawns. Therefore, in the fall or early spring, when the weather is generally best, homeowners start to think about improving the appearance of their lawns.

A Lawn in Fairly Good Condition

If your lawn is in reasonably good condition, and weeds aren't a problem, fertilize before the first flush of new growth begins in March (in central Florida), and then follow a regular watering schedule. Healthy lawns that receive proper water generally don't have to be fertilized more than once or twice a year. Some lawns require a fertilization in the fall to carry them through the winter.

Apply a good-quality lawn fertilizer to help your old grass green up and grow into bare spots. For best results choose a granular, controlled-release product high in nitrogen. If you have a serious weed problem, you might like to use a fertilizer that contains a weed control. These products, called herbicides, must be kept well away from trees, shrubbery, and flowers. They can cause damage by absorption through the roots or from drifts in the air.

A Lawn in Bad Condition

Restoring lawns takes water and fertilizer; filling in bare spots with new soil; resodding some areas and reseeding others; plus a lot of tender, loving care.

Soil preparation. If your lawn is in fairly bad condition, with bare spots, weeds, and thick, spongy thatch, you need to use a verticutter. This is a machine that loosens thatch and brings it to the surface, where it can be removed with a rake. Some lawn and spray companies offer this service, or the verticutter machine can be rented.

Give your weary lawn a once-over with the mower to even out its height and to remove brown grass tips. Vigorously rake out the thatch and other debris. Fill in low or bare spots with red dirt or good topsoil. Topsoil mixed with aged compost is an excellent base for a lawn. Whether you are planning to seed, sod, sprig, or plug, cultivate the soil several inches down in the bad areas with a spade to provide a suitable bed for root development. Filler soil should be loose, fertile, and free from stones and other debris.

Fertilizing. After the area is clean and level, apply a good-quality lawn fertilizer (6-6-6) according to the directions on the bag. It may be necessary to follow up in about six weeks with an application of a special type of fertilizer that is high in both nitrogen and potassium (the first and last numbers in the fertilizer ratio).

Shady areas on the north side of your home and under trees will require special attention. Areas that don't receive a lot of sun and are apt to stay too damp are more likely to develop fungus and diseases. It might be wise to apply a fungicide before replanting such areas if you suspect this might be part of your problem.

Choice of grass. Before planting new grass in shady areas, look up and see what might be done to let some sunshine through the trees. Pruning, thinning, and demossing can do wonders.

Refer to the section on lawn grasses (earlier in this chapter) when deciding which type of grass is best for your turf areas. When you buy sod, be sure it is free from weeds, insects, and diseases. It should be green and healthy. Inspect the undersides of the sod pads for grubs.

Watering. Try to keep your repaired areas evenly moist (but not too wet) until the new grass is firmly rooted. Water the old lawn from one to two inches every three days in the absence of normal rainfall. Early morning is considered the best time to water. Wilted blades and footprints on a lawn are signs that it's thirsty. To check on the amount of water that your sprinklers are putting out, place some small empty cans around the area or examine a plug of sod right after watering.

Run your sprinkler system through its complete cycle every week or two to check on faulty sprinkler heads. Hard water and salt air near the ocean mean constant maintenance. Also, ants like to set up housekeeping in sprinkler heads, where a drink of water is handy. This can block the water supply. Try to avoid overlapping sprinkler zones.

Thatch. The term *thatch* describes a lawn that is overfertilized, overwatered, and improperly mowed. Signs of thatch are a spongy lawn with brown, thick grass clippings piling up around and under the turf. Thick thatch holds moisture and keeps it from filtering down to roots, thus encouraging the invasion of fungus and disease. It also makes the lawn difficult to walk on and to mow.

However, it's wise to allow some grass clippings to fall back into the turf to supply nutrients. Clippings that fall back into the lawn should be short. If you let your grass get too tall between mowings, the clippings will be too long to filter down through the grass. Mulching mowers are a great help with this problem.

Some types of grass are more susceptible to this condition. St. Augustine seems to be the most vulnerable. It may be necessary to scalp your lawn in late February or early March and rake up the thatch. Then fertilize and keep the lawn watered properly so that it can recover.

Pests. Check to see if insects are causing some of your trouble. When in doubt, you should spray those areas (or the whole lawn) with the proper insecticide. There are also organic products that can be used successfully. See the section on organic gardening earlier in this chapter.

If you are not familiar with lawn-destroying insects and insecticides, call for professional help. See the section on establishing a new lawn earlier in this chapter. There are a number of spray companies that will examine your lawn and advise you free of charge.

The right time for lawn renovation. For spring renovation of your lawn, get busy in March. For fall renovation, start about the middle of September, while there is still a month to six weeks of active growing time left. Some grass that looks pretty hopeless will surprise you when it awakens from its dormant stage in spring or when the weather cools in the fall. An application of a complete fertilizer will speed this process.

Postfreeze Lawn Care

Many new residents become unduly concerned with the condition of their lawns following cold weather. Convinced that freezing temperatures have killed their grass, some have been known to pitch right in and replace their entire lawn with new sod.

To a degree, the extent of cold damage is determined by the general condition of your lawn. A lawn that has been properly planted, fertilized, watered, and mowed will undergo less damage than those that aren't as healthy.

But please don't panic. Although a lawn can be damaged by very low temperatures, it will probably not be killed. A number of turf grasses turn brown even in mild winter weather. The chances that yours will come back with proper care are very good. Don't resod prematurely.

Caution: The first cold spell causes Centipede grass to turn brown, and it will stay that way until spring. However, if only the tips of St. Augustine grass are burned by a freeze, these tips can be mowed off to expose the green grass underneath. By all means, don't lower your mower blades until late February or March, when the danger of frost is generally over.

Watering. There is very little one can do to protect a lawn from a hard freeze. Water well before and after the freeze. Wind and cold dehydrate lawns and plants, so they all require additional water.

Fertilizing. Spring fertilizing time differs depending on the general health of your lawn and your location. The idea is to feed your lawn sometime after the last anticipated freeze date and in time for it to take advantage of the vigorous growing season so that it will be in good condition before hot weather arrives. Central Florida gardeners generally choose March or April, depending on the weather conditions. Southern Florida gardeners can begin a few weeks earlier, northern Florida gardeners a few weeks later. This schedule has to be flexible because Florida winters are so variable.

Be assured that your winter lawn is not dead; it is only sleeping. Beneath the soil surface, the root system is slowly but surely feeding water and nutrients into the dormant buds. These will become plump and will rapidly push out new growth in the spring.

Antidote for a brown lawn. You may overseed the brown lawn with rye grass if you can't wait for nature to green it up. The kind of rye grass most often recommended for the Southeast is Oregon Annual, which will last until hot weather arrives in March or April. This rye does well in sun or shade, doesn't require rich soil, and withstands very cold weather.

Rye seeds may be sown by hand or by using a spreader. Broadcast five to ten pounds of seed per one thousand square feet of surface area. Rake lightly to get the seed through the old grass and into contact with the soil. If you desire, you may spread a very thin layer of topsoil over the lawn after sowing the seeds.

A fertilizer spreader can be used to apply the seeds when you don't have access to a regular seed spreader. Don't be concerned if you aren't able to spread these seeds evenly. Nubbin shoots will show within a few days. You can then go back over those areas that appear sparse or that you have missed. To ensure germination, keep the ground damp, not wet, by sprinkling.

Mow and fertilize only after the grass is well established—about two inches tall. A light application of a general fertilizer (6-6-6) will help maintain a nice green color and vigorous growth.

Rye grass is much brighter green than other grasses, so don't attempt to use rye just in bare areas or you will have a strange-looking, spotty lawn. However, on slopes or other places that have an erosion problem, a winter's growth of rye grass will help control this situation.

How to Mow a Lawn

Mowing time comes around too often, but there are things that can be done to simplify this chore so that you end up with a high-quality lawn. With proper design, equipment, and technique, mowing your lawn can become a chore you'll enjoy—and you'll have a lawn that's lovely to look at.

Design Suggestions for Lawn Areas

Foundation. Start by laying a firm foundation. Foundations for lawns should be soil with organic materials incorporated into the sandy topsoil. Low areas should be leveled and other grading defects corrected for ease of mowing and to prevent scalping.

Plan. Design lawn areas so they (1) are free of obstructions; (2) have curving corners that don't require slowing or backing the mower; and (3) have all curbs, stepping stones, and other paths at lawn level, so the mower can ride over them.

Avoid spotty planting of flowers, shrubs, and trees in lawn areas that interfere with your mowing pattern. Group plants requiring similar care.

Paving. Pave paths made by pedestrians who cut across the lawn. Paving materials can be bricks, asphalt, cement, pebbles, pine straw, marl, or stepping stones. Be sure to lay them on a firm base to avoid shifting.

Mulches or groundcovers. Use these between shrubs in groups, around bases of trees, between plants in a flower garden, or in shady areas where grass doesn't thrive.

The Right Equipment

Mowers. Select the lawnmower that suits your needs and your capability. Consider the different types of equipment available, the size of the area to be mowed, and the person who will be using the equipment. Recommendations: For less than half an acre, use a walk-behind mower. For one-half acre to one full acre, use a self-propelled, walk-behind mower or one of the highly maneuverable high wheelers. For more than an acre, you should probably use a riding mower or a tractor.

Self-propelled, walk-behind mowers require the operator to act only as a guide. The electric-cord mower is fine if your area is not too large and relatively level with few obstacles. Riding mowers yield a tangible savings in time. However, larger riding mowers sometimes have a powerful pull that can remove too much thatch and topsoil, thus causing damage to your lawn.

Remember, if you use a riding mower, you will probably also need a push mower to get into small spaces. Consider that a small mower for a large lawn or a large mower for a lawn with extensive plantings will prove inefficient. And take care to keep mower blades sharpened.

Line trimmer. For trimming places the lawnmower can't manage, you'll need a line trimmer. There are several types from which to choose, but it's crucial that you learn to use this tool correctly and exactly.

Tool recommendations. Keep all tools sharp and in good working condition. Organize your tool storage so that you never waste time looking for what you need. Buy good tools that will make using them easier. One high-quality tool will usually outlast three inexpensive ones.

Clothing. Wear proper clothing when mowing—gloves; sturdy, nonslip shoes; and long pants.

Procedures

Mowing height. Grass grows from its base, not its tip. Growing points are located at the crown (soil surface line above roots) rather than at the tips of the blade.

Do not mow too frequently or let the grass get too tall. The average lawn needs mowing every ten to fourteen days. This will depend upon the species of grass, the time of year, and weather conditions. Low cuts in hot weather let roots get burned by the sun. The average suggested mowing height is three inches. Removing more than one-third of the leaf surface in any one cutting reduces its ability to photosynthesize (manufacture the food necessary for the growth process). Mow grass in the shade slightly higher than grass in the sun.

Letting grass get too tall between mowings can cause other problems, such as blade and bag clogging. If grass has grown too tall, mow with the blade set high, lower the blade, and mow again. The height of the cut should never be drastically or suddenly changed.

Minimizing grass bagging. If you mow regularly and remove only about one-third of the grass blades, you can leave the catching bag off the mower and let clippings return to the lawn. If you find deep thatch building up, you are letting your grass blades get too long between mowings, cutting off too much each time, overfertilizing or over-watering, or all of the above.

Mowing wet grass. This results in an uneven cut and can clog the mower blades and the mouth of the bag. It is easier to cut dry grass, but never mow grass suffering from lack of water. Instead, water well, allow the blades to dry, and then mow.

Cutting patterns. For aesthetic purposes, alter cutting patterns with each mowing. That is, cut in an east/west direction once, then a north/south direction the next time, and diagonally the next. Make wide sweeping turns and avoid repeated turns over the same area. Mowing across hills, rather than up and down, is best for the grass.

Installing sprinklers. When installing a sprinkler system, it is wise to seek professional advice even if you plan to do the work yourself. Consideration of the mowing pattern is important. Avoid using many small sprinkler heads when one large one can cover the same area. Use the pop-up kind if the head has to be in the path of a mower. Try to avoid overlaps in zones because this causes some areas to receive too much water. Some relandscaping may be in order to avoid ob-stacles in the path of the mower.

GROUNDCOVERS

A lovely lawn is very nice, but there are areas where a green lawn is not practical. This could be a shaded section, such as the north side of a house or under a tree with dense foliage. Other places impracti-cal for lawns are slopes or hillsides, difficult corners, or areas that are too damp, hot, or dry. Nor does grass thrive where growing condi-tions are less than ideal because of foot traffic, poor soil, or exposure to high winds.

We usually think of groundcovers as low, rapidly growing plants that are dense enough to cover bare ground. However, various types of bark or mulch can also be used. Most groundcover plants can't tolerate being walked on but perform superbly in trouble spots. In general, groundcovers are easy to grow and require very little maintenance.

Choosing Plants

Selecting the type of groundcover for a particular spot depends on where your home is located and the type of terrain you have. If you live where salt is a problem and grass is difficult to grow, include salt-tolerant plants such as Algerian or English ivy, beach daisy (*Wedelia trilobata*), beach morning glory (*Ipomoea* spp.), coontie (*Zamia floridana*), dichondra, juniper, lantana, lily turf (*Liriope spicata*), mondo (dwarf lily turf, *Ophiopogon japonicum*), and ice plant (also commonly called Hottentot fig).

Several groundcovers can be used just as effectively as flowering annuals for spring, summer, and fall color. Another advantage is that most flowering groundcovers are perennials. For spring and summer flowering, consider ajuga (*A.* spp.), beach daisy (*Wedelia trilobata*), bromeliad, coleus, Confederate jasmine, day lily, dwarf marigold, dwarf azalea, dianthus, gazania daisy, heather, impatiens, kalanchoe, lantana, moss rose, natal plum (*Carissa* spp.), periwinkle (*Vinca* spp.), strawberry begonia, sweet alyssum, verbena, wax begonia, wedelia, and yellow jasmine. Heather, lantana, verbena, and wedelia can provide year-round color.

Some of our most popular all-green foliage covers are dichondra, English and Algerian ivies, ferns, juniper, lily turf (*Liriope* spp.), mondo grass (monkey grass, dwarf lily turf), spider plant, pachysandra, and peperomia (*P.* spp.).

Plants that can produce a novel effect include bromeliad, oyster plant or Moses-in-the-Bulrushes (*Rhoeo discolor*), purple heart or purple queen (*Setcreasea* spp.), and several wandering Jews (*Zebrina* spp.). However, all of these can be damaged or killed by frost.

Two plants used for groundcovers and commonly spoken of as ferns are *Asparagus sprengeri* and coontie (*Zamia floridana*), but they are actually not members of the fern family. Both are relatively frost-tolerant.

Attractive ferns used for groundcovers are Boston, bracken (wild native), holly (*Cyrtomium falcatum*), leather leaf, and maidenhair (*Adiantum cuneatum*).

Plants recommended for dense shade include Algerian or English ivy, cast-iron plant (*Aspidistra elatior*), dichondra, ferns, mondo grass, mosses, spider plant (*Chlorophytum* spp.), and wandering Jew (*Zebrina* spp.). Liriope thrives in shade but blooms better with some sun.

Planting

Spacing your plants depends on the kind you select. Vigorous plants such as junipers may need three to four square feet. Smaller ground covers can be spaced six inches apart when a quick, dense cover is desired. Periwinkle and ajuga should be planted eight to twelve inches apart. If you overplant, it is easy to go back later and thin the area. It's usually best to be patient and wait for growth instead of planting too close. The best time to plant is spring or fall, not in the hot months.

It is essential, before planting, to prepare the soil properly. The area should be dug and then the soil loosened and enriched with compost and a balanced garden fertilizer.

Planting on slopes requires specific care to avoid erosion. Collars, rocks, netting, or a special mulch can be used to hold the soil. Discuss this problem with someone familiar with landscaping.

Caring for Groundcovers

Control weeds in groundcover by hand until your plants have had time to produce a thick carpet.

The growth rate of the groundcover can be used to determine the amount of fertilizer to apply. A complete fertilizer such 6-6-6 or 8-8-8 applied in spring and midsummer is adequate for most groundcovers.

Water requirements vary with different plants. The best rule to follow is to learn the water requirements of specific plants and water when needed.

Groundcovers Most Popular for Seacoast Planting

Ajuga (*A.* spp.). Ajuga has deep green, purple, or bronze leaves that are slender and shiny. With adequate sunlight all varieties turn iridescent purple-bronze in the fall. In spring, ajuga displays clusters of small blue, purple, red, or white blossoms. These low-growing plants spread rapidly in sun or shade, but are a lot more colorful in the sun.

Algerian ivy (*Hedera canariensis*). This ivy has very large green leaves but a tendency to grow rather sparsely. In order to encourage bushier growth when using it as a groundcover, keep stray branches pruned off and shear the vines rather severely in the spring. This ivy does best in deep shade and on slopes. It is salt-tolerant.

Asparagus (*A. sprengeri*). This groundcover offers durability, drought resistance, color, and texture for the landscape. It also boasts a strong root system and bears lovely, soft, white flowers in the summer followed by bright red berries in the fall. It will tolerate full sun but has better dark green color in the shade. New growth is a lovely lime-green color.

Beach daisy (*Wedelia trilobata*). This is a trailing perennial with some dark and some light green leaves. It thrives in sun or shade but blooms best in full sun. When planted in the shade, it has a tendency to reach for the sun and thus grows out of bounds. Beach daisies love the sandy soil along the dunes and bear bright yellow flowers most of the year. They can be damaged by frost but usually come back in the spring. Propagate by rooting cuttings.

Dichondra (*D. micrantha*). This tiny evergreen vine is not a grass but makes a lush, dense, lime-green carpet. It has round, cup-shaped leaves that resemble small lily pads. Dichondra grows very low to the ground. It does best in semishade in moist areas. Dichondra can freeze down but will come back. It rarely requires mowing and spreads by runners. Seeds are available.

English ivy (*Hedera helix*). Generally seen as a clinging vine, this plant works beautifully as a groundcover due to its compact growth and small, dark green, shiny leaves. English ivy is easy to propagate by cuttings and spreads rapidly after getting established. It is salt- and cold-tolerant and prefers shade and cool places. If it starts to get unsightly or out of control in a few years, set your mower high and mow it off. Fertilize and water it well, and it will come back.

Gazania daisy (*G.* spp.). This daisy is sun-, drought-, and wind-resistant and will grow in any type of soil. It is low spreading and blooms continually, with flowers of many colors on the same plant—red, yellow, orange, pink, white, ruby, violet, brown, and cream. Gazania daisies are excellent ground-covers for seacoast gardens.

Ice plant, Hottentot fig (*Carpobrotus edulis*). This succulent, with its soft, grayish-green, spiky leaves, is an excellent groundcover for the seacoast. Large daisylike, yellow to rose flowers appear in the spring. They are followed by a fruit that resembles a fig but is not edible. The plant is a rapid grower that endures heat, drought, and salt spray and will thrive in any type of soil that offers good drainage. Ice plants are especially recommended for slopes.

Juniper (*Juniperus* spp.). Several species of juniper make good ground-covers. Some lie flat while others grow to sixteen inches in height. They all tolerate drought, sun, wind, extremes in temperature, and lack of fertilizer. Shore juniper (*J. conferta*) is especially good as a groundcover, with a low, spreading growth pattern and tolerance of salt spray. The worst enemy of junipers is the spider mite. These insects can be destroyed with a pesticide spray if you recognize them early.

Lantana (*L. montevidenesis*). Considered native to Florida, this hardy, trailing plant makes a good groundcover because it will tolerate poor soil, hot sun, drought, and salt spray. Lantana blooms profusely, with deep lavender or white flowers most of the year. It is good for slopes.

Liriope, creeping lilyturf (*L.* spp.). Lily turf's half-inch wide leaves don't like too much heat but can be grown in part sun or shade to reach twelve to eighteen inches in height. Variegated varieties grow too tall to use as groundcovers but are excellent for borders. A slow grower, this plant will eventually start producing blue flowers on spikes, followed by black berries in summer. Little care is required because liriope tolerates a wide range of soil conditions, such as drought, lack of fertilizer, and light salt spray. Liriope can be high-mowed in early spring. Propagate by seeds or division of clumps.

Maidenhair fern (*Adiantum* spp.). This fern has tiny, wiry stems with lacy, delicate leaflets. Older growth is dark green, but new growth is a lovely shade of light green. Fronds in all stages of development add to its beauty. The soil should be kept evenly moist. Maidenhair has a dormant period in winter when less water is required but should not be allowed to dry out completely. This fern likes light but not direct sun. It multiplies by underground roots and has a tendency to spread away from bright light (from south to north). Its delicate leaves should be protected from windy areas and salt spray. Maidenhair can freeze down in winter but will come back in the spring. Rich soil and fertilizer don't seem to be necessary for good health. Plants are excellent for slopes or rock gardens.

Mondo grass, monkey grass (*Ophiopogon japonicum*). Also known as dwarf lily turf, this plant is related to liriope but grows only six to ten inches high and has slender leaves. Small blue flowers on short spikes are followed by blue berries. Little care is required because mondo grass tolerates a wide range of soil conditions, such as drought, lack of fertilizer, and light salt spray. Propagate by seeds or division of clumps. The plant can be high-mowed in early spring.

Moss rose (*Portulaca grandiflora*). This succulent has narrow, fleshy leaves and produces a profusion of flowers that come in a myriad of bright colors. The flowers open every morning in the sunshine and close in cloudy weather. They prosper in hot, dry locations; do well in rather poor soil; and tolerate salt spray as far back as the second dune line. Propagate by seeds, which should be sown monthly for continuous blooms because the blooming period lasts for only a few weeks.

Pachysandra (*P. terminalis*). This prostrate evergreen herb makes a dense mass and is an excellent groundcover for seaside plantings. Saw-toothed leaves grow in clusters, and small spikes of white flowers appear above the leaves, sometimes followed by white berries. The plant likes light to deep shade and needs rich, moist, slightly acid soil. Propagate by divisions or rooted stem cuttings.

Periwinkle (*Vinca rosea*). Periwinkle is a very hardy old standby. It is a fast, vigorous grower in almost any type of soil. A bright, upright plant from six to eighteen inches tall, periwinkle has glossy green leaves and flowers in all of the Easter shades—white, pink, blue, lavender, and yellow. Plants can withstand some salt spray and are maintenance-free.

Purple Heart, Purple Queen (*Setcreasea purpurea*). This trailing plant has deep purple, lance-shaped leaves that complement its lavender flowers. It grows well in almost any soil, in sun or shade. Plants bloom profusely in the morning, but the flowers close in the afternoon. Purple Heart is easy to root from cuttings.

Spider plant (*Chlorophytum* spp.). These plants grow in dense clumps of narrow, curving leaf blades that are solid green or striped with white or cream. The plantlets grow on stems that "spider" out from the mother plant, extending in all directions. Each new plantlet develops vigorous, bulbous roots, which makes them easy to snip off and plant. Spiders like morning sun or high shade. They are lovely as houseplants in pots or hanging baskets.

Verbena (*V.* spp.). Several species of this annual or perennial herb appear in places near the sea and along the Gulf Coast in the South. They are prized for their showy flowers, which come in shades of white, pink, blue, lavender, rose, red, and yellow. They prefer sun and are drought-resistant. Propagate by seeds or division.

Wandering Jew (*Zebrina pendula*). This fast-growing, spreading succulent is available in a variety of forms such as all green, purple, or white velvet; others are variegated with stripes of green with white or green with cream. The sprawling foliage is very attractive and is easily rooted. The color of the small flowers varies with the variety. Wandering Jews are tolerant of almost any type of soil that is well drained. They will freeze but will usually come back. They are not salt-tolerant.

Redesigning Your Landscape

This section will give you a general outline to follow if you have moved into an older home that needs perking up or if your landscaping is old and has become overgrown. The emphasis is on simplicity of design and ease of maintenance. With planning, it's possible to have an attractive and functional landscape that does not require constant maintenance.

I. Observation

A. Take an overall look at your yard from a distance. If your house is near the street and you want to create depth illusion:
  1. Leave open spaces on the sides of the house so that you can see beyond, especially if you are on the water.
  2. Carefully place some plantings between the house and the street to help the house recede into the background.
  3. Plants with a blue cast near the house give an illusion of distance.
  4. Graduate plants according to size to give a vista effect (larger near the street to smaller near the house.)
  5. Take advantage of open spaces for flowing lawns.

B. Next, examine individual areas in your yard. Decide which to leave, which to improve, and which to eliminate entirely. What effect do you want to achieve?
  1. Try to blend (be in harmony) with your neighborhood in color of home, flowing lawns, and plantings. A brightly painted house on a street with soft colors is seldom attractive. Hedges and fences delineating each house produce visual unrest. A very formal garden stuck between two informal or natural settings seldom achieves success.
  2. Decide whether you want to emphasize your house or play it down.
  3. The shape of the house, lot, and existing plantings dictates the overall design.
  4. Decide which areas are to be public and which private, the uses of these areas, and the needs of the family.
  5. Decide on focal points such as the front door, a specimen tree, a colorful shrub, a rock, a fountain, a lily pond, a flower bed, or a garden.
  6. Enhance views seen from inside the home.

II. Drawing

A. Make a simple drawing showing the house, driveways, trees, major plants, and flower beds. Use a piece of thin tracing paper over this outline and move things around until you get the desired effect.

1. Get rid of the clutter. Avoid a scattered arrangement of flower beds, trees, and garden accessories. Eliminate as many frills as possible. A good design is based on simplicity. Open lawns and groupings of plants that require similar maintenance are generally more effective.
2. Then decide which plants you want to use. This will be a compromise between what you like and what will do well in your particular circumstances.

III. Plants

A. Don't overplant (that is, don't crowd and don't plant more than you can take care of).
B. The first consideration is supplying adequate water and proper drainage.
C. Are plants of your choice cold-, wind-, and salt-hardy? If you use tender plants, place them in containers or planters, on a patio, or in some area where they can be protected from high wind and cold.
D. Learn the type of soil in various areas in your garden, and the type of soil and fertilizer each plant requires.
E. Be familiar with the growth habits of plants you choose, such as rate, mature size, and general shape.
F. Learn the color and texture of your plants at different seasons and stages of growth: color of bloom, size of leaves, evergreen or deciduous. Avoid spots of color but concentrate it in mass beds or borders. Stick to a few colors that blend. Remember that annuals require high maintenance.
G. Find out whether your plant requires full sun, semishade, or full shade and which exposure is best. The northern side gets the least sun. Group plants according to similar needs (don't mix sun and shade, wet and dry).

IV. Placing plants

A. Avoid "under-the-overhang" and "all-around-the-foundation" plantings. Foundation plantings should build up the corners, soften and frame a home. Place low-growing plants under windows and larger plants against larger wall surfaces. You may frame the house with larger plants or trees. A flat roof may be enhanced by tall, spreading trees. Place good-quality plants at the front door and other conspicuous areas. Use an unusually beautiful or interesting plant as a focal point.

B. The balance may be symmetrical or asymmetrical. Using matching pairs of plants on each side of the front door or driveway is difficult. They rarely ever grow and develop in an orderly fashion. Perhaps a larger one on one side and three smaller graduated ones on the other would be a better solution. If one side of the home is higher than the other, follow the lines (place higher and larger plants on the side with the greater mass and lower growing plants on the other side). Graduate larger plants down with smaller ones, such as from tree to shrub to flower, or border to groundcover or lawn.

V. Maintenance

A. This requires proper tools in good condition. The basics are three pairs of clippers (hand, long-handle loppers, long-blade hedge shears), two sizes of trowels (wide and narrow), three shovels (round point, square, and narrow spade), two rakes (one light and flexible for leaves, one with metal tines for heavier work), and a curved handsaw.

B. For easier maintenance replace a flat-clipped hedge with one that looks more natural.

C. Replace some lawn with groundcovers, pavement, or gravel.

D. Avoid creating areas that require edging. Where edging is necessary along walks or curbs, eliminate shrubbery. If you desire a border, use border grass (liriope, mondo) or shrubbery that isn't too close to the ground (hollies, low junipers).

E. Avoid surface slopes that are steeper than a one-foot rise in a two-foot run because slopes are difficult to mow. Use some groundcovers instead of all lawn.

F. Avoid fast-growing plants such as elaeagnus, some bamboos, and pyracantha unless needed for a particular purpose.

G. Learn to prune properly!

H. If a plant isn't doing well after a reasonable time and effort, move it or replace it. Love your plants; don't fight with them. On the other hand, let them know who's boss.

I. Use mulches to aid in moisture retention and weed control.

VI. Trees

A. Trees offer more than aesthetic beauty. They are noise, dust, wind, and heat shields; visual screens; a frame for the house; protection for shade plants; and homes for birds and squirrels.

B. You should know the characteristics of your trees, such as their root systems (surface or deep), whether they're evergreen or deciduous, their ultimate size and growth rate, whether they cause litter, and the seasonal color of their foliage and flowers. The root systems of maples and cypress will destroy your lawn and break your driveways and walkways.

C. Use smaller trees or large shrubs for small lots and leave larger trees for large lots. Overgrown shrubbery can sometimes be pruned into charming small trees. Emphasize the form of the tree and use the nice shapes of trunks and limbs.

D. If there are too many trees, study them, take out the lesser ones, and shape the rest. Groundcovers can be added under trees in conformity with existing landscape. Thin trees with heavy foliage to allow some sunshine to come through.

E. Grading around trees properly is crucial to saving their lives. There is a balance between the root system and the crown that should not be disturbed. If roots are destroyed, then some foliage must be pruned away. If roots are exposed, build a box around the tree to keep soil from washing away. In areas where the water table is near the surface, trees are shallow-rooted. Without deep taproots, they don't have strong support and can be blown over by the wind. Surface roots need air to breathe; so when you fill around a tree, you are taking a chance of killing it. To be perfectly safe, don't disturb soil any closer to the trunk than the drip line. It's best to plant trees far enough from the house so that limbs don't hang over the roof and drop leaves in the gutters or cause wind damage.

VII. Other landscape components

A. Learn to use rocks properly or don't use them! Rocks should appear to be a natural part of the earth, such as an outcropping or a boulder, not an explosion in a rock quarry. It is more refined and tasteful to use too few than too many.
B. Structural components such as curbs, walks, arbors, small accessory buildings, pools, benches, and tables should relate to the building materials used in the house as well as its type of architecture and color. Fences require less maintenance than hedges and occupy less space.

References for Landscaping

Libraries have many good reference books on landscaping. Here are three that I have found most helpful throughout the years:

Menninger, Edwin A. *Seaside Plants of the World*. Hearthside Press, 1964.
Watkins, John V., and Thomas Sheehan. *Florida Landscape Plants*. Gainesville: University Press of Florida, 1975.
Watkins, John V., and Herbert S. Wolfe. *Your Florida Garden*. Gainesville: University Press of Florida, 1978.

CHAPTER 5

❀

Garden Calendars

Planting times indicated in this chapter are not precise but are based on the average conditions for central Florida. Northern Florida gardeners generally plant a couple of weeks later; southern Florida gardeners plant a couple of weeks earlier. If you will observe the suggestions in the following sections, you will learn the right time for most chores as well as what and when to plant each month.

JANUARY

January weather is unpredictable. It may be mild, or the temperature can drop below freezing. Extreme temperatures usually last for only a few hours, but they can persist for several days. As a rule, the ground does not freeze. In general, two hard freezes are the most we can expect to endure in January and February.

Planting

Annuals. Choose African daisy, bachelor's button, calendula candytuft, California poppy, cornflower, dianthus, forget-me-not, gladiolus, Johnny-jump-up, larkspur, pansy, petunia, Queen Anne's lace, snapdragon, statice, stock, strawflower, sweet alyssum, and sweetpea.

Perennials. Choose dusty miller, chrysanthemum, gaillardia, gazania daisy, hollyhock, and Shasta daisy.

Vegetables. Green, leafy ones are the hardiest—beets, cabbage, celery, collards, endive, English peas, kale, mustard, salsify, spinach (winter varieties), lettuce (Bibb, Black-Seeded Simpson, Buttercrunch, Prizehead, Salad Bowl, Romaine, Great Lakes), and turnips. Also choose broccoli, Brussels sprouts, carrots, cauliflower, kohlrabi, leeks, onion seeds and sets, parsnips, Irish potatoes, radishes, rutabaga, and Swiss chard. Butter beans, peppers, and tomatoes can be planted year round with protection from frost.

Fruits. Choose grapes and strawberries.

Herbs. Choose oregano, basil, chives, dill, marjoram, and parsley. Plant them in pots to be moved indoors in case of a freeze warning.

Grasses. Choose winter rye for lawns, liriope and mondo for borders.

Ferns. Choose *Asparagus sprengeri*, coontie, and holly.

Palms. Pindo (*Butia capitata*), sago (*Cycas revoluta*), lady (*Raphis excelsa*), date (*Phoenix canariensis*), *Phoenix reclinata*, and cabbage (*Sabal* spp.) are the hardiest; but all can be freeze-damaged.

Trees. Celebrating Arbor Day, America's official tree-planting day, is important because of our growing environmental concerns. National observance of the day is usually on the last Friday in April, but the state of Florida has designated the third Friday in January to call attention to the value of trees and to encourage their planting.

I would like to see Florida change this date to March or April to be closer to the onset of the spring rains and the growing season. January weather in central and northern Florida is usually cold and windy and not conducive to planting trees. (See table 1 in chapter 3.)

Hardy Plants

Evergreen shrubs. Choose arborvitae, ardisia, boxthorn, camellia, elaeagnus, euonymus, fatsia, gardenia, holly, India hawthorn, juniper, ligustrum, nandina, photinia, pittosporum, podocarpus, pyracantha, viburnum, and wax myrtle.

Foliage plants. Choose ardisia, some bamboos, some bromeliads, cast-iron plant (*Aspidistra elatior*), *Philodendron selloum*, and yucca.

Flowering shrubs. Choose azalea, bridal wreath, camellia, crape myrtle, dogwood, fruit trees, gardenia, India hawthorn, oleander, and rose-of-Sharon.

Vines. Choose Carolina and Confederate jasmine, grape, ivies (English, fig vine, and Algerian), and wisteria.

Roses. Container-grown and bare-root roses can be planted now, but it is best to wait until February or March. Keep up your monthly watering, spraying, and light fertilizing routine even though your roses are probably not producing many blooms at this time.

Chores

Poinsettias. These will freeze if the temperature goes as low as thirty-two degrees.

It's a good idea to have on hand some old blankets and corrugated boxes to cover plants in case of a freeze warning. If you use plastic, be sure it doesn't touch the foliage, and remove it before the sun hits the next morning. A light bulb beneath the covers will keep temperatures a few degrees warmer. Heavy mulching will help protect root systems.

Planning ahead. Don't forget to make New Year's resolutions. Resolve to begin a compost pile, use organic fertilizers, and use a self-mulching lawnmower. Plan to stop overwatering, overfertilizing, and overplanting. Try to learn the proper way to prune. Be more conscientious about recycling. Use more xeriscape and native plants, and practice conservation when possible. Exercise restraint in the use of pesticides, and learn to use organic methods of gardening. And stop procrastinating and take care of garden chores when it is time!

FEBRUARY

If the winter has been mild you can expect violets, bush daisies, and narcissus to bloom this month.

Mid-February is considered the average last frost date, but the Atlantic coast can get at least one hard freeze in February or March.

Cold air dehydrates plants as much as hot weather does, so continue a regular watering schedule.

Planting

Annuals. Choose African daisy, ageratum, aster, candytuft, calendula, California poppy, coreopsis, dianthus, forget-me-not, Johnny-jump-up, larkspur, lobelia, Mexican sunflower (*Tithonia rotundifolia*), pansy, periwinkle, petunia, Queen Anne's lace, strawflower, snapdragon, statice, stock, sunflower, sweet alyssum, and touch-me-not (balsam).

You can choose from several species of snapdragons: butterfly with flared petals, long-stemmed ones with single flowers, taller varieties for background, or dwarf ones for borders. When snaps get nipped by frost, they can be pinched back. This stimulates branching, which produces fuller bushes with more blossoms.

Perennials. Choose chrysanthemum, dusty miller, gaillardia, hollyhock, lantana, Shasta or gazania daisy, and verbena.

Bulbs. Those that have lost leaves from a freeze should be fine if they are growing in soil that drains well. Cut yellowing and browning leaves off at the ground level. Bulbs need a rest period. Now is the time to plant precooled tulips; however, tulips are not recommended for warm climates.

Vegetables. Choose green, leafy ones such as beets, cabbage, celery, collards, endive, kale, lettuce (Bibb, Black-Seeded Simpson, Buttercrunch, Prizehead, Salad Bowl, Romaine), mustard, and spinach (winter varieties). You can also plant beans (bush, butter, lima, and pole), broccoli, Brussels sprouts, carrots, cauliflower, corn, eggplant, kohlrabi, leeks, onion seeds and sets, English peas, Irish potatoes, radishes, rutabaga, squash, and Swiss chard.

Eggplant, English peas, peppers, and tomatoes need protection from frost.

Fruits. Choose cantaloupe, grapes, and strawberries.

Herbs. Plant seeds of your favorites in pots on a sunny windowsill (basil, chives, rosemary, mint, parsley, sage, sweet marjoram, and thyme). They can be transferred to the garden in the spring.

Trees. See table 1 in chapter 3 for hardy trees that can be planted now. Plant citrus and Florida varieties of apples, figs, grapes, peaches, and pears.

Chores

Azaleas. The most hardy are known as Southern Indian (*Azalea indica*), of which the most popular are the Formosas.

Keep your azaleas watered well. Mild winters confuse azaleas, causing them to pop a few blooms here and there well before their normal blooming time. They need cold spells to allow for a dormant period. Unless frost destroys their buds there should be spectacular displays toward the end of March. Add new plants during the blooming period in order to be sure of color choice. The best time to plant new ones is in the spring during the blooming period so that you can choose colors that are harmonious.

Pruning. Late February is considered the best time to prune roses, cutting them back one-third to one-half.

Grapevines should be pruned at this time, if there has been enough cold weather to allow dormancy. Be sure to cut back to firm, springy wood and leave about three main leaders. If the weather warms up and your grapevines sprout, it will not hurt the vines should the new growth be killed by a freeze. Grape clusters grow from buds formed on last year's wood and not on the long trailing terminals that develop in the spring.

No other pruning of shrubs needs to be done at this time except to remove dead wood. If there should be a hard freeze, do not prune damaged parts until spring.

Watering. Gardening along any seacoast, where plants are subject to sandy soil, salt spray, wind, and erratic rainfall, requires proper management of water. Water as needed in the absence of rain. If there is salt in your well water, rinse plants and flush soil with city water after using sprinklers and after windy days.

Planning ahead. This is a good time to start getting ready for your spring garden. Get your lawnmower and tools sharpened; prepare soil;

turn and compost beds; and plan what, how many, and where to plant when spring comes.

See you in March!

March

March is a month of contrasts—cold, hot, windy! Gardeners never know just how to plan for their spring gardens. Severe winters generate a lot of necessary cleanup, but mild winters can encourage early spring planting. In any event, get busy and have the earliest spring garden possible. Generally, toward the end of the month almost anything can be planted.

Planting

Annuals. Chose ageratum, aster, baby's breath, calendula, candytuft, carnation, coleus, celosia, bachelor's button, cockscomb, coreopsis, cosmos, daisies, forget-me-not, globe amaranth, gourds, impatiens, larkspur, lobelia, marigold, moss rose, nasturtium, pansy, periwinkle, petunia, purslane, phlox, salvia, snapdragon, sunflower, strawflower, sweet alyssum, touch-me-not (balsam), wishbone flower (*Torenia fournieri*), and zinnia.

Perennials. Choose begonia, black-eyed Susan, chrysanthemum, dahlia, dusty miller, gaillardia, gazania daisy, geranium, gerbera daisy, glory bower (*Clerodendrum* spp.), hibiscus, kalanchoe, lamb's ears, lantana, liriope, rose-of-Sharon (mallow), salvia, sedum, Shasta daisy, society garlic, sweet alyssum, and verbena. Divide clumps that have become crowded.

Vines. Choose Carolina and Confederate jasmines, roses, and wisteria.

Bulbs. Choose lily-of-the-Nile, amaryllis, Amazon lily (*Eucharis grandiflora*), blood lily, caladium, calla, canna, crinum, dahlia, day lily, gladiolus, gloriosa, Louisiana iris, rain lily, and spider lily (*Hymenocallis keyensis*).

Vegetables. Choose beans (bush, butter, lima, and pole), beets, bell peppers, broccoli, Brussels sprouts, cabbage, carrots, collards, corn, cauliflower, cucumbers, eggplant, endive, Irish potatoes, kale, kohlrabi, lettuce (Bibb, Black-Seeded Simpson, Buttercrunch, Prizehead, Salad Bowl, Romaine), leek, mustard, okra, onion sets, peas (black-eyed, Texas Cream 40, White Acre, Zipper Cream), pumpkins, radishes, salsify, squash, spinach (New Zealand), sweet potatoes, tomatoes, and turnips.

Fruits. Choose apples, cantaloupe, citrus, grapes, honeydews, papaya, peaches, pears, and watermelons.

Herbs. Choose anise, basil, borage, chives, dill, fennel, ginger, lemon balm, lemon grass, marjoram, mint, oregano, parsley, peppers, rosemary, sage, savory, sesame, and thyme.

Shrubs for flowers. Choose allamanda, angel's trumpet, ardisia, azalea, beauty berry, bridal wreath, camellia, cassia, carissa, flowering fruit trees, gardenia, hibiscus, India hawthorn, ixora, plumbago, pyracantha, and roses.

Trees and Shrubs

See tables 1 and 2. Crotons, chenille plant, hibiscus, ixora, Jacob's coat, and copper leaf need protection from frost.

Flowering. Choose bottle brush, buckeye, cassia, crape myrtle, dogwood, golden rain, holly, loblolly bay, magnolia, mimosa, oleander, orchid tree (*Bauhinia* spp.), Jerusalem thorn, and wild plum (hog). Also choose citrus and Florida varieties of apricot, apple, peach, pear, and plum.

Evergreen. Choose arbor vitae, bay (red and loblolly), bottlebrush, camphor, cedar, cherry laurel, holly (American, dahoon, East Palatka, Burford, and yaupon), loquat, magnolia, pine, and palm.

Deciduous. Choose crape myrtle, cypress, dogwood, golden rain, hickory, maple, Jerusalem thorn, redbud, sweet gum, and sycamore.

Hardy evergreen shrubs. Choose arborvitae, boxthorn, camellia, cedar, elaeagnus, euonymus, fatsia, gardenia, holly, India hawthorn, juniper, ligustrum, nandina, viburnum, pittosporum, podocarpus, photinia, and wax myrtle.

Foliage Plants for Fall Color

Trees. Choose ash, cypress, Chinese tallow (popcorn), dogwood, elm, hickory, maple, mulberry, sassafras, sycamore, sweet gum, redbud, and tulip.

Shrubs. Choose chenille plant, copper leaf, croton, nandina, photinia, and Virginia creeper vine.

Chores

Poinsettias. When outdoor plants lose leaves and become leggy, cut them back twelve to eighteen inches from the soil line—eight inches for smaller plants. If flowers are still pretty, continue to enjoy them and prune later. Plants in pots should be transplanted into slightly larger pots or planted in the ground. Choose a location with full sun, protected from wind, and where no light will reach them at night. Water well about twice a week and fertilize lightly (6-6-6) now, in June, and again in late fall.

Pruning. The usual advice at this time is to wait until the middle of the month to start pruning. But this will depend upon the severity or mildness of the winter. Mild winters produce lush growth on evergreens, and tiny buds appear early on many flowering plants. Should you prune away these buds, there won't be as many flowers. You can remove some of the winter's growth on evergreen plants. Even if we should get a freeze this late, most plants won't have time to put out new growth before the spring growing season that could be damaged.

Most spring-flowering shrubs should be pruned after their blooming period is over. Newly planted or transplanted trees and shrubs generally need to have some foliage tip trimming done to compensate for loss of roots during digging. Root pruning can be done on plants that you are planning to transplant in a month or six weeks. This stimulates the main ball to produce new feeder roots.

Spraying and fertilizing. An application of a balanced fertilizer with minor elements for lawn and shrubbery at this time will help them get a good start for their spring growing season. Although 6-6-6 ratio has been most popular, recent research recommends 16-4-8 with minor elements for general fertilization purposes. Plants that don't appear in good condition might be helped by a nutritional foliage spray. Use an acid fertilizer on azaleas, camellias, gardenias, and crotons. Reapply several inches of organic compost (mulch) to almost all plants to help control weed growth and hold moisture throughout the hot summer. Be alert to pests and disease such as leaf miners, aphids, thrips, whiteflies, worms, and fungus as the weather warms up. Spray as necessary.

Soil. Keep building up compost piles. For quicker breakdown, keep pile moist, but not soggy, and turn every few weeks.

Roses. Plant bare-root or container-grown bushes. Be sure to buy only those on rootstock adapted to your area. Florida root stock should be Dr. Huey or *Rosa fortuniana*. Keep up a regular water, fertilizer, and spray program.

Planning ahead. March is an important gardening month. Don't take any shortcuts on soil preparation. Rework to a depth of ten to twelve inches and add new compost, manures, and an organic fertilizer. Sharpen and repair your tools, or get some new ones. They will pay for themselves in time because they will speed up your work and make it a lot more pleasant. If you give this month your devoted attention, your rewards will be great the rest of the year.

April

April is generally a lovely spring month that entices us to spend time outdoors. Azaleas, redbuds, dogwoods, spireas, gardenias, violets, bougainvillea, and Confederate jasmine vines are starting to bloom.

Planting

Annuals. Choose coleus, celosia, bachelor's button, cosmos, daisy, dianthus, globe amaranth, gourds, impatiens, marigold, moss rose, aster, periwinkle, phlox, purslane, salvia, sunflower, strawflower, sweet alyssum, touch-me-not, verbena, wishbone flower, and zinnia.

Perennials. Choose begonia, black-eyed Susan, bush daisy, butterfly weed, chrysanthemum, dusty miller, four o'clock, gaillardia, gazania daisy, geranium, gerbera daisy, glory bower, hibiscus, kalanchoe, lamb's ears, lantana, liriope, rose-of-Sharon, salvia, sedum, Shasta daisy, and verbena.

Bulbs. Choose lily-of-the-Nile, amaryllis, Amazon, blood lily, caladium, canna, crinum, day lily, gladiolus, gloriosa, and rain lily.

Vegetables. Choose beans (butter, lima, and pole), carrots, collards, corn, cucumbers, eggplant, gourds, lettuce (Bibb, Black-Seeded Simpson, Buttercrunch, Prizehead, Romaine, Salad Bowl in high shade), mustard, okra, onion sets, peas (black-eyed, English, Texas Cream 40, White Acre, and Zipper Cream), peppers, pumpkins, radishes, rutabaga, New Zealand spinach, squash, sweet potatoes, tomatoes, and turnips.

Fruits. Choose banana, citrus, grape, peach, pear, papaya, cantaloupe, honeydew, and watermelon.

Herbs. Choose anise, basil, borage, chives, dill, fennel, ginger, lemon balm, lemon grass, mint, marjoram, oregano, parsley, sage, sesame, summer savory, and thyme.

Shrubs. Plant trees and shrubs for year-round color, such as azalea, bottlebrush, camellia, cassia, crabapple, crape myrtle, gardenia, golden rain, hibiscus, hydrangea, India hawthorn, Jerusalem thorn, oleander, orchid trees, photinia, plumbago, redbud, rose-of-Sharon, spirea, and viburnum.

Florida varieties of fruit trees such as peach, plum, pear, crabapple, and apple flower beautifully in the spring.

Palms. You can plant or transplant palms at anytime of the year, but April through June is best. They require tremendous amounts of water until well established. Hardy ones include pindo (*Butia capitata*), Chinese fan (*Livistona chinensis*), sago (*Cycas revoluta*), saw cabbage (*Paurotis wrightii*), date (*Phoenix canariensis*), Senegal date (*P. reclinata*), lady (*Raphis excelsa*), cabbage (*Sabal* spp.), saw palmetto (*Serenoa repens*), windmill (*Trachycarpus fortunei*), and Mexican fan (*Washingtonia robusta*).

Chores

Lawns. This is the time to get to work on your lawn. See the sections on lawns in chapter 4.

Roses. If you pruned, sprayed, and fertilized your roses as instructed last month, you should have nicely shaped bushes with lush foliage at this time. Remove old and new canes that don't seem strong. Container-grown roses can be planted almost anytime except in extremely cold weather. March and April, before the weather gets warm, are generally ideal months to plant bare-rooted ones. Keep them watered well; soak new plants with water at least every other day. Avoid wetting the foliage.

Pruning. Prune as necessary to remove dead wood, suckers, and weak branches; to eliminate any branch that crosses and rubs against another; and to maintain proper shape. Cut poinsettias back if you haven't already done so. Repot in larger pots or plant in the ground. Fertilize with 6-6-6 and keep watered.

All flowering shrubbery should be pruned after the blooming period. Mulch well for the spring and summer.

Rejuvenate old liriope and pampas grass by cutting low to the ground. Fertilize and water well.

Spraying. Diseases and insects arrive with warm weather and new spring growth. Be on the lookout and spray before worms, aphids, spider mites, mealybugs, whiteflies, thrips, and scales get a head start on you. See the section on garden pests in chapter 2.

Houseplants. Move them outdoors into the shade for recuperation after being shut in all winter. Scrub off any signs of salt build-up on the outside of pots. Add new soil to the top of pots, gently working it in around the root system. When indicated, divide, repot, and add new soil. Cut back weak and leggy parts of plants to encourage new growth.

For extra color, plant some hanging baskets and pots that can be moved around to brighten areas. All containers should have drainage holes for best results.

MAY

If we have had those customary April showers, May should be an ideal month for gardeners. The cool, breezy days are delightful, and the weather is perfect for working in the garden. Magnolia, wisteria, mimosa, and crape myrtle are starting to bloom.

This is our last chance to get major chores done before hot weather makes working out of doors not quite so pleasant. Any major planting should be done right away, or you should wait until cooler weather next fall.

Planting

Annuals. Choose ageratum, calendula, celosia, coleus, cockscomb, cosmos, daisy (African, gloriosa), dianthus, four o'clock, globe amaranth, gaillardia, gourd, impatiens, marigold, morning glory, moss rose, nasturtium, ornamental pepper, periwinkle, phlox, purslane, strawflower, sunflower, touch-me-not, verbena, wishbone, and zinnia.

Perennials. Choose begonia, black-eyed or green-eyed Susan, butterfly-weed, daisy (bush, gerbera, gazania, and Shasta), dusty miller, geranium, glory-bower, hibiscus, hollyhock, kalanchoe, lamb's ears, lantana, liriope, phlox, purslane, roses, rose-of-Sharon, salvia, sedum, and verbena.

Geranium, gazania daisy, black-eyed Susan, sweet alyssum, and verbena can be grown as annuals or perennials.

Try cascading begonias, lantana, moss rose, nasturtiums, sweet alyssum and verbena in hanging baskets or elevated planters. If you have winter/spring petunias that are waning, sheer them back, fertilize, and dust with a pesticide, and you will get some summer bloom.

Vines. Choose black-eyed Susan, bleeding heart, bougainvillea, Carolina and Confederate jasmines, coral (*Antigonon leptotus*), cypress, grape, Hawaiian bridal, honeysuckle, hoya, ivy geranium, flame (*Pyrostegia ignea*), ivies (*Hedera* spp., Algerian, English, and creeping fig), mandevilla, Mexican flame (*Senecio confusus*), *Monstera deliciosa*, morning-glory, nasturtium, passion flower, philodendron, Virginia creeper, roses, wisteria, and yellow allamanda.

Bulbs. Choose caladium, canna, crinum, gladiolus, gloriosa-lily, and rain lily.

Vegetables. Choose beans (butter, lima, and pole), bell peppers, carrots, collards, cucumbers, eggplant, lettuce (Buttercrunch, Salad Bowl in high shade), mustard, okra, onion sets, peas (black-eyed, Texas Cream 40, White Acre, Zipper Cream), pumpkins, radishes, rutabaga, squash, New Zealand spinach, sweet potatoes, tomatoes, and turnips.

Fruits. Choose banana, cantaloupe, citrus, papaya, watermelon, and loquat.

Herbs. Plants that will tolerate the summer heat include basil, chives, dill, lemon balm, lemon grass, marjoram, mint, oregano, parsley, peppers, rosemary, sage, and thyme.

Shrubs and trees. See the March calendar.

Palms. Palms can be planted almost anytime of the year if given copious amounts of water for the first few months until new roots are well established. See the April calendar.

Roses. Container bushes can be planted anytime, but it's getting too late for bare-rooted ones. Spray regularly with a fungicide/pesticide about every two weeks. Fertilize once each month if plants are in good condition. See the section on growing roses in chapter 3.

Chores

Diseases and pests. Warm weather promotes new, tender growth, which becomes a prime target for insects and diseases. Start your control early. Spray at the first sign of invasion. The use of a combination insecticide/fungicide product simplifies this chore. Shrubs with large leaves are especially susceptible to worm and grasshopper damage. The most effective grasshopper control is to hand-pick and destroy them quickly before they multiply. The little black ones are the new generation of the big yellow-red ones. A copper spray is effective for fungus.

Fertilizing. You should have fertilized your lawn and all shrubbery by this time. Use a general 6-6-6 balanced fertilizer on most plants according to the instructions on the package. The amount per plant depends upon the size and health of the plant. If your soil is sandy, light applications monthly are more effective than heavy applications less frequently.

Azaleas, camellias, crotons, and gardenias need a special acid-producing fertilizer such as Camellia/Azalea Special. All plants grow better with the addition of some organic material to the soil (compost, manures, and peat). If you have a tendency to overfertilize, use an organic product to avoid burning the roots of plants. If you wish to force more bloom, use a fertilizer with a high second number (phosphorus) or a light application of superphosphate.

Watering. During some years we are short on rainfall in the spring, so keeping things watered properly is of major importance. Water, fertilizer, and warm weather help things grow rapidly.

Lawn care. Start a new lawn or renovate an old one. See the sections on lawns in chapter 4.

Mowing. It's very important to understand the correct way to mow your lawn. See the section on mowing in chapter 4.

Pruning. Finish pruning as soon as possible. Complete necessary pruning for dead wood and for controlling the size and shape of plants. Prune azaleas, camellias, and gardenias after their blooming period is over. Now is a good time to do air layering and to root cuttings.

Composting. Replenish your compost piles with clean leaves, grass clippings, layers of soil, manures, fireplace ashes, and kitchen scraps. Use materials that break down easily to form new soil for your garden. Keep the pile slightly damp, and turn with a pitchfork about once a month. Compost deteriorates more rapidly in warm weather.

Stop, look, and listen to nature. You don't want to miss many of life's treasures.

JUNE

We can generally expect cool breezes and temperatures in the eighties in June, which makes gardening very pleasant. However, the weather can get even warmer.

Planting

Hot-weather annuals. Choose gaillardia, geranium, impatiens, marigold, periwinkle, moss rose, purslane, salvia, sunflower, verbena, and zinnia. Keep plants well watered and remove spent blossoms to stimulate continuous bloom.

Perennials. Choose begonia, black-eyed Susan, gaillardia, gazania daisy, geranium, lantana and verbena. It is not too late to pinch back perennials that have become spindly.

Vegetables. Choose beans (butter, green, and lima), bell peppers (sets), collards, corn, cucumbers, eggplant, leeks, mustard, okra, peas (black-eyed, Texas Cream 40, White Acre, Zipper Cream), pumpkins, radishes, rutabaga, New Zealand spinach, squash, sweet potatoes, tomatoes, and turnips.

Vines. Choose black-eyed Susan, bleeding-heart, bougainvillea, Carolina and Confederate jasmines, coral, cypress, grape, Hawaiian bridal, honeysuckle, hoya, ivy geranium, flame (*Pyrostegia ignea*), ivies (Algerian, English, and creeping fig), mandevilla, Mexican flame (*Senecio confusus*), *Monstera deliciosa*, morning glory, nasturtium, passion flower (may-pop), philodendron, Virginia creeper, roses, wisteria, and yellow allamanda.

Fruits. Choose banana and papaya. Bananas may ripen all summer if given adequate water, fertilizer, and deep mulch. Peaches and blueberries should be ready for harvesting.

Herbs. Choose basil, chives, coriander, dill, fennel, lemon balm, lemon grass, marjoram, mint, oregano, parsley, peppers, and rosemary.

Colorful foliage plants that tolerate hot weather. Choose caladium, coleus, copper plant, croton, and Joseph's coat.

Chores

Houseplants. Increase watering and feeding during this active growing period. A liquid fertilizer sprayed on the leaves can give plants a boost. A plant may need to have new soil added or be moved up to a slightly larger container.

Some houseplants benefit by going outdoors for a few weeks or the whole summer. Dieffenbachia, ferns, peperomia, philodendron, rubber plants, and Swedish ivy must stay in the shade, but cacti, succulents, and most foliage plants can gradually be moved into filtered or morning sunlight.

Propagation. Now is an ideal time to air-layer and make root cuttings of plants such as azalea, croton, hibiscus, ivies, and oleander. Many plants can be rooted by bending a cane over, covering a segment with soil, placing a brick on top of the soil, and keeping the soil moist until roots develop. The new plant is then cut from the mother and replanted in a pot or in the ground. Azaleas, roses, most vines, coleus, and impatiens can be propagated in this way.

Warm-weather tips. In the years that we experience a shortage of water, curtail the purchase of new plants accordingly. Select hardy, hot-weather varieties. See the section on xeriscaping in chapter 2.

Learn the water requirements of your particular lawn. Don't overwater. See the sections on lawns in chapter 4.

Roses. Keep up a regular fertilizer program, with intervals of two to three weeks. When the weather gets hot, taper off. Insects, scales, and fungi get to be a greater problem in hot weather. Keep a close watch and spray as indicated. Keep plants watered well; avoid letting roses dry out completely. See the section on roses in chapter 3.

Fertilizing. Inexperienced gardeners should use an organic fertilizer that will not burn the foliage or roots. Wet the soil, apply the fertilizer, and then water it in. In sandy soil along the seacoast, it is better to use several light applications at about six-week intervals rather than one heavy application. If chlorosis (paleness) appears on the foliage of plants, spray with an iron sulfate or a solution of chelated iron. General use of an acid fertilizer is a good idea in sandy alkaline soil. Foliar spray feeding is an easy method and gets speedier results.

Poinsettias. Cut back according to how well they are growing and how tall you want them to be for the Christmas season. They may not need cutting back now if they are bushy; but if they are leggy, cut them twelve to eighteen inches from the ground. Keep watered, and fertilize about three times a year—spring, summer, and fall.

Pests. Watch closely for hot-weather invasions of chinch bugs, armyworms, fungus, aphids, thrips, various worms, grasshoppers, scales, and mole crickets. Learn to recognize these pests and ask someone at your nursery to recommend the best method of eradication. Follow instructions carefully and get to work at the first signs of trouble.

Enjoy June—it's one of our nicest months. Lots of flowers are blooming, such as hydrangeas, oleanders, and gingers. Sultry July is on the way, so get your major chores completed before the real hot weather arrives.

July

The people you hear singing about "those lazy days of summer" aren't gardeners! Now's the time we have to work hard to help our gardens survive the very hot months.

Planting

Annuals. Choose calendula, coleus, dianthus, impatiens, marigold, periwinkle, salvia, and zinnia. Remove spent flowers, or blooming will decline because the strength of the plant will go toward developing seeds instead of producing new flowers. Cutting stems off with the faded flowers will stimulate most annuals to branch and produce more buds.

Perennials. Choose dusty miller, gaillardia, lantana, moss rose, and verbena.

Vegetables. Choose bell peppers, celery, collards, eggplant, Jerusalem artichokes, okra, peas (black-eyed, field, crowder, White Acre) pumpkins, rutabaga, spinach (New Zealand), squash, sweet potatoes, and tomatoes.

Chores

Water. The amount of water depends upon the kinds of plants, the type of soil, and weather conditions. Check the soil in a plant's root zone to see if it's wet or dry. If it's dry, water. If it's moist, don't water. Overwatering is as bad for plants as inadequate water. Keep plants well mulched and apply less fertilizer in the hot months.

Lawn care. This is especially crucial during hot weather. A green lawn makes summer days seem a little cooler. A lawn is badly in need of water when the blades look wilted and their edges start to curl. Another sign is footprints left on the grass when it is walked on. The best time to water is early morning, when temperatures are cooler and there is usually less wind. Water thoroughly when needed instead of giving the grass frequent light sprinklings.

Keep mower blades sharp and set them a little higher. Grass blades need to be long enough to shade roots.

Keep a sharp eye out for lawn insects and diseases. Chinch bugs arrive with warm, dry weather. Damage usually appears as a patch with a dead center and a yellowish margin. Examine the yellow-into-green margin areas for tiny (red, black, or gray) chinch bugs scurrying away rapidly. See the section on establishing a new lawn in chapter 4.

Pests. Spray and dust plants as indicated (especially roses). Diseases, insects, and fungi are more troublesome in hot weather. Start your spray program before the infestation is serious. See the section on garden pests in chapter 2.

Going on vacation. Before leaving on a trip, place houseplants in an area that receives good light but not direct sun. Most plants can survive a two-week span if watered thoroughly before you depart. Pots resting on a tray of pebbles with water in the bottom of the tray will help supply humidity. The bottoms of pots should not touch the water.

Fertilizing. Apply less fertilizer, and use organic in hot weather. Organic fertilizer won't burn your plants. Wet the soil, fertilize, and water in. Mulch heavily around plants to help keep roots cool, decrease evaporation, discourage weeds, and add organic material to the soil.

Roses. Roots of roses should be soaked with water at least every third day unless there is a great deal of rainfall. When watering, avoid wetting the foliage because this encourages the development of fungi and disease. Black spot is especially rampant in warm weather. Keep up your regular spray program. Use light applications of fertilizer during the hot months. Keep spent blossoms removed, fallen leaves picked up, and the area free of weeds. Keep well mulched, adding more mulch as necessary. See the section on roses in chapter 3.

Pruning. Hot-summer pruning should be limited to dead wood, water sprouts, and thinning. However, flowering trees and shrubs should be pruned after they stop blooming.

Weeding. Do a thorough weeding job. Weeds that are allowed to go to seed will make this problem more difficult later. Weeds steal moisture and nutrients and spread diseases and fungi. Plant cover crops in bare ground and turn them under in the fall to discourage weeds and help enrich the soil. Good summer cover crops include several varieties of peas, rye grass, clover, and sweet potatoes. Organic gardeners refer to these crops as *green manure*.

Harvesting. Keep all ripened fruit and vegetables picked. If you are going away, make a deal with a friend to water and harvest the garden in exchange for the fruits and vegetables collected.

Propagation. Make cuttings or air-layer your favorite ornamentals such as abelia, althea, azalea, bottlebrush, coleus, crape myrtle, croton, gardenia, hibiscus, ligustrum, oleander, and poinsettia.

Other maintenance suggestions. Pinch tips off chrysanthemum plants to induce branching and thus more blooms in the fall. Fertilize every few weeks until flower buds appear.

Keep flower buds removed from coleus and caladium so that all their vigor can go into providing attractive foliage.

Take care of gardening chores in the early hours of the morning or late afternoon to avoid the heat. Priorities for hot weather are watering, weeding, mowing, and spraying.

August

The most important aspect of gardening at this time of year is to supplement rainfall with adequate water. Even in shade, hot, dry winds can soon deplete moisture. Plants with large leaves such as hydrangeas, coleus, and caladiums require more water than plants with small leaves. Next spring's azalea and camellia buds are forming now, so don't let lack of moisture damage them.

Planting

Annuals. Plant ageratum, calendula, coleus, cosmos, marigold, periwinkle, snapdragon, stock, sunflower, and zinnia in seed flats. A few plantlets are available: chrysanthemum, coleus, gerbera daisy, purslane, salvia, and verbena. Summer flowering plants should have old blossoms and excessive growth trimmed and receive a light application of fertilizer. Mums and daisies will branch and bloom again.

Perennials. Begonia, blue salvia, gaillardia, moss rose, lantana, and mallow can be planted in seed flats.

Vegetables. Collards, cucumbers, eggplant, loosehead lettuces, okra, peppers, squash, and tomatoes can be planted now in seed flats but must mature before frost. Some plantlets of collards, peppers, and tomatoes are available.

Cold-hardy vegetables. Broccoli, Brussels sprouts, cabbage, cauliflower, celery, collards, endive, mustard, radishes, romaine, rutabaga, New Zealand spinach, squash, and turnips can be planted in seed flats.

Seed flats should be placed in filtered shade and kept moist. A shading canopy of burlap, cheesecloth, or lathes is a good way to cut down on moisture loss. Remove as soon as plants are growing well.

Bulbs. Dahlia and gladiolus tubers set out now should produce flowers within three months. Plant more every few weeks to extend the season.

Most day lily pods are ripe when they turn brown, and the seeds can be planted. These seeds won't keep in storage for more than six months.

Leave gloriosa-lily seed on the vine until the pods burst; then gather them and plant.

Chores

Fruits. Ready for harvest are apples, grapes, Kieffer (sand) pears, and pecans. Harvest pears before they are quite ripe.

Roses. These are blooming out and resting. Treat each rosebush as an individual. Water, prune, and fertilize according to need.

Poinsettias. These should be cut back for the last time about the middle of August to ensure early bloom for Christmas. The extent of pruning will depend upon the size of plant you desire at blooming time. Pruning produces bushier plants for more blossoms. If your plants are growing well and you prune now, they will probably grow about three feet between now and November. Make cuttings from the hardwood you cut off. Soft cuttings won't root. Be alert for insect invasion on new growth. Spray and fertilize monthly. See the section on poinsettias in chapter 3.

Crape myrtle. Flowering stems should be removed after the blooming period is over. If you let them go to seed, strength needed for growth and foliage will be sapped from the plant.

Camellias and gardenias. If too many buds appear on one stem, some should be pinched off to prevent overloading the branch. The remaining flowers will be larger and more beautiful.

Insects and diseases. These are at their worst in August. A tan appearance, brown edges, or curling leaves are signs of trouble. Look for lacebugs on undersides of pyracantha, sycamore, and elm leaves. Watch for worms on undersides of oleander and bougainvillea leaves. Keep an eye on the lawn for armyworms and chinch bugs. Spray at first evidence before these pests get a head start. Spray peaches, pears, apples, and citrus for scab and scale. Watch for aphids on tender, new growth on ornamentals.

Citrus. New growth needs special care such as spraying with a copper fungicide when the leaves look crinkly and rusty and with a pesticide when there are signs of insects such as aphids, grasshoppers, moths, cutworms, red spiders, and whiteflies. Additional nutrients can be supplied by spraying with a solution containing minor elements. Both a light application of Citrus Special fertilizer and adequate water are important at this time.

Soil. If you prepared the soil well for your spring garden, it will probably not need as much attention now. Work in compost, manures, and some well-balanced fertilizer. Cultivate occasionally to prevent a weed problem and to help aerate. It is always a good idea to use a mulch.

Hot-weather scheduling. In August, take care of your gardening during the early morning hours and cool off in the ocean during the day.

September

It's possible to have four gardens a year in the southeastern part of the United States. In order to accomplish this, you must begin this month. Many people start their fall gardens as early as August; however, extremely hot weather in September makes that a risky practice.

New gardeners should plan a small garden in order to learn as they go and be able to keep up with the many necessary tasks—watering, fertilizing, weeding, spraying, mulching, and staking. It's possible to have a productive garden in a very small space. A plot too large will become a chore and lead to discouragement.

Two efficient methods for dooryard gardens are using raised beds and combining attractive vegetables with flowers in beds and borders. Raised beds can be made from cross-ties, stones, concrete blocks, or boards as well as by mounding. This method concentrates plantings and eliminates some stooping. See the section on vegetable gardens in chapter 4.

Planting

Annuals. Choose African daisy, ageratum, bachelor's button, calendula, candytuft, celosia, coleus, coreopsis, cosmos, dahlia, dianthus, forget-me-not, impatiens, lobelia, marigold, nasturtium, pansy, periwinkle, salvia, snapdragon, statice, stock, strawflower, sunflower, sweet alyssum, and zinnia.

Perennials. Choose begonia, black-eyed Susan, blue salvia, chrysanthemum, daisy (African, gerbera, Shasta, gloriosa, and gazania), dusty miller, gaillardia, geranium, hollyhock, moss rose, sedum, and verbena.

Bulbs. Choose lily-of-the-Nile, amaryllis, calla, canna, crinum, Easter, ginger, gladiolus, gloriosa, blood lily, day lily, spider lily, Louisiana iris, narcissus, and rain lily for spring flowering. Tulips and daffodils are not recommended for warm climates. See the sections on bulbs in chapter 3.

Old clumps of lilies that have become large and crowded should be dug and divided at this time. Day lilies should be replanted immediately, but large amaryllis bulbs can be stored in a cool, dry place for a couple of months. Remove small bulbs and replant immediately.

Some caladium bulbs can be left in the ground year round if the soil is well drained. Otherwise, dig; allow bulbs to dry out; shake off soil; spread in a single layer in a flat box; dust with pesticide; and store in a cool, dry place where they won't freeze until it's time to set them out next March.

Vegetables. Vegetables recommended for fall planting include beets, broccoli, Brussels sprouts, beans (bush, lima, and pole), cabbage, carrots, cauliflower, celery, collards, cucumbers, eggplant, endive, green peppers, kohlrabi, leaf lettuce, leeks, mustard, onions, radishes, salsify, winter spinach, winter squash, Swiss chard, and tomatoes. If you're more experienced and want a larger variety, add English peas, kale, and Jerusalem artichokes.

However, the following vegetables are tender and have to be planted early because they need to be harvested before frost: beans (bush, lima, and pole), cucumbers, eggplant, green peppers, winter squash, and tomatoes.

As long as the weather is quite hot, it's best to start seeds of beets, broccoli, Brussels sprouts, cabbage, cauliflower, celery, collards, endive, kale, kohlrabi, leeks, mustard, onions, spinach, and Swiss chard in flats where moisture, warmth, and oxygen can be controlled.

Vegetables that can be started from seeds sown directly into the ground are bush beans, carrots, cucumbers, English peas, radishes, and turnips.

When planting onions, it's best to wait until the weather is cooler and buy sets (young sprouts). Onions, garlic, and marigolds planted in a scattered arrangement will help deter insects.

There are a large number of tomato varieties from which to choose. A half-dozen plants will supply the average family. Plant the kind that suits your needs for canning, stewing, or table use. Miniature tomatoes are easy to grow and make nice hanging baskets. It is possible to have fresh tomatoes year round if you choose the correct varieties and plant them in the right sequence.

Leaf lettuce planted in partial shade is a good choice for the warmer fall months. Plant several kinds such as kale, endive, Romaine, and spinach for interesting salads.

Chores

Roses. Roses need special attention in the fall. Enrich beds with compost and manures, mulch heavily, and fertilize once each month. While enriching beds, keep in mind that roses have shallow, spreading roots. Prune moderately to remove all dead wood and spindly branches. Shorten main canes and lateral branches that have become too long. Leave the major pruning until February. Add new container-grown plants in October, November, and December. It's best to wait until spring to plant bare-root specimens.

Poinsettias. It's getting too late to prune poinsettias if you expect to have good color well before Christmas. If you cut them back in the summer, it may not be necessary to prune at this time. This will depend upon how tall you want them at Christmas. Vigorous, healthy plants will grow from two to three feet between now and flowering time. Pruning controls the size of your plant and stimulates growth that produces branching. The more terminal shoots produced, the more colored bracts you have. Fertilize with 6-6-6. Poinsettias are short-day/long-night plants that need uninterrupted dark to set flowers properly; therefore, do not plant near artificial light. See the section on poinsettias in chapter 3.

Chrysanthemums. Pinch the buds off heavily laden plants so the remaining flowers will be larger and more beautiful.

Azaleas and other flowering shrubs. These should receive a light application of fertilizer to see them through the winter.

Summer annuals. Cut off spent flowers from leftover summer annuals to encourage bloom well into fall. Save seeds when possible for spring planting, but keep in mind that seeds from hybrids will not reproduce true.

This month enjoy the beautiful goldenrain trees and bougainvillea vines in bloom.

October

October is a prime month for planting. Shrubbery and trees planted now have proven to do well because there is time for roots to get established before the active spring growing season.

Balled-and-burlapped or container-grown plants are recommended rather than bare-rooted ones. Essentials for success include planting before cold weather is expected, mulching well, applying adequate water, and protecting plants from severe cold when it arrives.

Do some fall planting now to help reduce the hectic deluge of spring gardening chores.

Planting

Annuals. Choose baby's breath, bachelor's button, calendula, candytuft, carnation, coreopsis, dahlia, delphinium, dianthus, daisy, impatiens, lobelia, larkspur, nasturtium, ornamental cabbage, kale, petunia, pansy, Queen Anne's lace, snapdragon, statice, stock, strawflower, sweet alyssum, sweet pea, sunflower, and verbena.

Perennials. Choose begonia, black-eyed Susan, blue sage, chrysanthemum, daisy (African, gerbera, Shasta, gloriosa, and gazania), dusty miller, gaillardia, geranium, hollyhock, poppy, sedum, and verbena. Old clumps of perennials should be dug and divided every few years. Dust or spray for mildew and insect control.

Bulbs. Choose lily-of-the-Nile, amaryllis, calla, canna, crinum, Easter, ginger, gladiolus, gloriosa, blood lily, day lily, spider lily, Louisiana iris, narcissus, society garlic, and rain lily for spring flowering. See the sections on bulbs in chapter 3.

Vegetables. Seeds that should be started in flats and then transplanted into the ground are broccoli, Brussels sprout, cauliflower, collards, eggplant, endive, kale, kohlrabi, spinach (winter varieties), squash, Swiss chard, and tomatoes. Seeds that can be planted directly in the ground are bush beans, cabbage, carrot, celery, cucumber, English peas, leeks, lettuce (Bibb, Black-Seeded Simpson, Buttercrunch, Prizehead, Salad Bowl, Romaine), mustard, onion, radish, rutabaga, salsify, and turnips.

Fruits. October is strawberry planting time. Prepare rich soil with good irrigation, separate old plants and replant, plant new ones, and fertilize every five weeks. It's best to plant on slightly elevated hills or in raised beds. Try some in hanging baskets or a strawberry jar.

Herbs. Seeds to start in flats include basil, caraway, marjoram, mints, oregano, parsley, rosemary, sage, and thyme. Transplant into the garden in about a month if the weather remains mild.

Roses. It's best to plant container-grown ones now. Old bushes are tired and need a rest by this time of year. If you didn't prune last month, do so now. Fertilize well, add new organic material (compost, manures, and peat), apply two to three inches of mulch, and continue your regular spray program. See the section on roses in chapter 3.

Lawns. Correct soil problems and then plant new grass or seeds. Plant winter rye grass as soon as the weather turns cool. See the section on helping your lawn recover in chapter 4.

Hydrangeas. These can be planted now. They should have been pruned soon after blooming. Remove any lower limbs that are drooping on the ground. The more acidic the soil, the bluer the flowers.

Foliage plants for fall color. Plant your own Indian summer using *Acacia farnesiana*, *Ardisia crenata*, *Acuba japonica*, *Nandina domestica*, *Cassia bicapsularis*, *Plumbago capensis*, firethorn, copper leaf, croton, dogwood, golden rain, hickory, maple, orchid (*Bauhinia variegata* or *B. blakeana*), sycamore, cypress, holly, and ginkgo.

Virginia creeper vine is a rampant grower and produces large, bright red leaves in the fall.

Chores

Pruning. Prune only to remove dead wood and to shape evergreens and deciduous plants. Citrus trees need selective pruning. See the section on pruning in chapter 2.

Fertilizing. Use a light application for the lawn, fruit trees, and tender plants such as azalea, camellia, croton, gerbera, hibiscus, holly, and ixoria. Use a fertilizer with low nitrogen (the first number) to help plants harden off (get ready for cold weather). Apply chelated iron for yellowing leaves on evergreen foliage.

Preparing for Christmas. In order to set blooms, poinsettias and Christmas cacti need short days and long nights at this time of year. Keep them away from any artificial lights.

A Christmas cactus should be put in a darkened place for a dormant rest for about three weeks in October. Don't fertilize or water during this rest period. Then bring it out, place it in good light, water, and lightly fertilize. It's best not to move the plant again until after the blooming cycle is complete. Changing the environment will sometimes cause flowers to drop. If moving is necessary, do so while buds are still closed. Rotate pot every few days during blooming period for uniform exposure to light.

The correct amount of water seems to be the most crucial part of growing these plants successfully. Treat them like a true cactus by keeping them slightly on the dry side. If they are too wet, they will rot at the soil level. If your plant is healthy, the stems will be dark green and fleshy. If the stems look wrinkled, that is a sign of dehydration. If your plant doesn't bloom for Christmas, it may be an Easter cactus, or it's blooming cycle may be upset by unusually warm fall temperatures.

November

This is the month to enjoy Indian summer and the tinge of fall in the air. Shorter days and cooler temperatures trigger trees to drop their leaves. The manufacture of chlorophyll ceases, unmasking chemicals that result in brightly colored foliage. The depth of the color can depend on the amount of sunshine striking the leaves. This is one explanation for patches of varying hues on the same tree.

Planting

Annuals. Choose African daisy, ageratum, aster, baby's breath, bachelor's button, calendula, California poppy, candytuft, carnation, celosia, coreopsis, daisy, delphinium, dianthus, forget-me-not, larkspur, lupine, nasturtium, pansy, petunia, Queen Anne's lace, salvia, statice, snapdragon, stock, sunflower, strawflower, sweet alyssum, sweetpea, touch-me-not, and verbena.

Dianthus, dusty miller, pansy, snapdragon, and stock are the most cold-hardy. The others will need some protection in the event of a freeze. Ornamental cabbage and kale are colorful, cold-hardy, and edible.

Snapdragons planted now may be cold-damaged. If so, snip them back to stimulate branching for an abundance of spring blossoms.

Perennials. Choose black-eyed Susan, chrysanthemum, daisy (gerbera and Shasta), dusty miller, gaillardia, hollyhock, liriope, and rose-of-Sharon. It's not too late to divide old clumps of perennials.

Bulbs. Choose lily-of-the-Nile, amaryllis, calla, canna, crinum, Easter, ginger, gladiolus, blood-lily, day lily, spider-lily, Louisiana iris, narcissus, rain lily, and society garlic. Narcissus planted now will usually bloom in January or February if the bulbs are mature. Narcissus bulbs should be dug and replanted about every five years.

Vegetables. Choose green, leafy ones such as beets, broccoli, cabbage, collards, endive, kale, leeks, lettuce (Black-Seeded Simpson, Buttercrunch, Salad Bowl, Prizehead, Romaine), mustard, salsify, spinach (winter varieties), and turnips. Also choose Brussels sprout, carrots, cauliflower, celery, English pea, kohlrabi, leeks, onion sets, radish, Swiss chard, and tomatoes. Lettuce, bell peppers, eggplant, and tomatoes planted now will need protection from frost.

Fruits. Plant strawberries.

Herbs. Plant basil and parsley.

Flowering shrubs. Plant or transplant azalea, butterfly bush, camellia, gardenia, hydrangea, powder puff, spirea, and viburnum. Plant hardy trees at this time. It's best to choose container-grown stock. Wait until March for more tender varieties to allow them a summer's growth before cold weather.

Vines. Choose bougainvillea, Confederate jasmine, ivies (Algerian, English, and creeping fig), *Mandevilla splendens*, passionflower (maypop), Virginia creeper, and wisteria. Bougainvillea blooms in the fall and throughout mild winter months.

Lawns. Rye grass can be sown over established lawns at five pounds of seed per one thousand square feet. If your lawn is in good condition, you may not need to fertilize until spring. Otherwise, fertilize lightly with a balanced product. Set mower blades higher and mow less often.

Foliage plants for fall color. If your garden doesn't include foliage that treats you with fall color, plant *Ardisia crenata, Acuba japonica, Nandina domestica, Cassia bicapsularis, Plumbago capensis,* firethorn, copper leaf, croton, dogwood, goldenrain, hickory, maple, orchid (*Bauhinia variegata* or *B. blakeana*), sycamore, cypress, holly, ginkgo, and Virginia Creeper vine.

Chores

Roses. Keep up your regular monthly schedule of feeding, spraying, and mulching. Use lighter applications of fertilizer during the winter months. Increase in March when the active growing season is approaching. Keep plants watered well, but avoid wetting the leaves. If you pruned properly last month, you should have healthy new foliage at this time. Plant only container-grown bushes now. Wait until spring for bare-root specimens.

Odd jobs. Prune dead wood only, weed, add mulch, build up compost piles, and enrich soil in beds with well-seasoned compost and manures. Fertilize citrus trees at the rate of one pound per foot of tree spread.

If the foliage on your poinsettias is not dark green, give them a light application of a general fertilizer or spray with a liquid fertilizer. Watch for pests on new, tender growth. See the section on poinsettias in chapter 3.

On chrysanthemums, snip off spent flowers to encourage branching for a bushier plant and more blossoms.

Potted plants should be moved to protected areas in case of a freeze warning. Repot them if they seem to be pot-bound or in need of improved soil.

Christmas cacti should bloom well if you allowed them to rest in October. See the October calendar.

Get your fall chores completed so that you can enjoy the holiday season.

DECEMBER

Generally, December presents ideal circumstances for gardening—cooler weather, rainfall, and warm sunshine. We don't expect really cold weather until at least January. However, there have been years when we are hit with a hard freeze before Christmas. Most plants need some cool nights in the fall in order to become dormant (slow down their growth and get some rest).

Plant some winter bloomers to help perk up the garden on gloomy winter days. You'll need a location for blooming plants that gets at least six hours of sun each day. The soil should have a pH of about 6.8 (slightly acid) and should contain enough compost, peat moss, sand, and manures to nourish and give adequate drainage. Be alert to weather conditions and cover plants in case of a freeze warning.

Planting, Weather Permitting

Annuals. Choose ageratum, aster, bachelor's button, California poppy, candytuft, carnation, calendula, coreopsis, forget-me-not, daisy, dianthus, strawflower, larkspur, lupine, pansy, petunia, Queen Anne's lace, salvia, snapdragon, sweetpea, statice, stock, sweet alyssum, and verbena. Dianthus, dusty miller, pansy, snapdragon, stock, and sweet alyssum are the most cold-hardy.

Perennials. Choose black-eyed Susan, chrysanthemum, dusty miller, gaillardia, gerber daisy, hollyhock, liriope, mallow, rose-of-Sharon, and Shasta daisy.

Bulbs. Choose lily-of-the-Nile, bugle lily (*Watsonia* spp., gladiolus family), amaryllis, calla, canna, crinum, dahlia, Easter, gladiolus, spider-lily, Louisiana iris, narcissus, rain lily, and society garlic. Louisiana iris planted now may not bloom until its second spring. Mature narcissus bulbs should bloom in late January and February. For satisfactory bloom, amaryllis should be planted with one-third of the bulb above the soil line.

Vegetables. Choose green, leafy ones such as beets, cabbage, carrots, cauliflower, celery, collards, endive, kale, kohlrabi, lettuce (Bibb, Black-Seeded Simpson, Buttercrunch, Prizehead, Salad Bowl, Romaine), mustard, spinach (winter varieties), and turnips. Also choose bell peppers, broccoli, Brussels sprout, English peas, Irish potatoes, leeks, onion seeds and sets, parsnips, radishes, rutabaga, Swiss chard, and tomatoes. Bell peppers, eggplant, and the lettuces will do well during a warm winter but need protection in case of a frost warning.

Fruits. Plant strawberries.

Herbs. Plant basil and parsley.

Flowering shrubs. Choose acacia, allamanda, azalea, butterfly bush, camellia, cassia, gardenia, hydrangea, natal plum, oleander, plumbago, spirea, and viburnum.

Vines. Choose bougainvillea, Confederate jasmine, coral, honeysuckle, *Mandevilla splendens,* and wisteria. Bougainvillea bloom in the fall and throughout mild winter months.

Trees. Plant any hardy ones. See table 1 in chapter 3.

Roses. Plant only container-grown ones now. Wait until late February and March for bare-rooted ones. Keep up your regular water and spray program. Water well every three to five days, but decrease the amount of fertilizer during the winter months. Spray with a combination fungicide/insecticide every two to three weeks.

Lawns. Rye grass can be sown over established lawns (five to fifteen pounds of seed per one thousand square feet). To avoid having a spotty lawn, don't plant rye in bare areas only. Set the mower higher and mow less often.

Chores

Fertilizing. Feed blooming plants monthly with a slow release, high-phosphorus product (the middle number on the fertilizer bag). Phosphorus promotes blooms.

Watering. Plants require more water in very cold weather due to dehydration and lack of rainfall. In the absence of rainfall, soak lawns well once or twice each week. Frequent light sprinklings are not recommended. If you receive notice of an impending freeze, water plants and lawn well before and after the cold spell.

Poinsettias. Plants should have developed colorful bracts by this time. Keep watch for insects that chew new tender leaves.

Chrysanthemums. Prune the spent flowers after blooming to encourage branching that will produce a bushier plant and more blossoms.

Houseplants. Provide adequate lighting and good drainage for indoor plants. Mist foliage occasionally except those plants with fuzzy leaves. Keep out of drafts, away from heaters and lights that burn all night. Group pots, or place them on a tray containing water and filled with pebbles, to help keep the humidity balanced. Pot bottoms should not rest in the water.

Christmas cactus. Plants should bloom well if you gave them a rest period in October. Don't move a plant after the buds start to open because the blossoms have a tendency to drop with a change of environment. The pot should be rotated every few days to give all sides equal exposure to light.

General care. Prune dead wood only, remove weeds, add mulch, build up your compost pile, and enrich the soil with well-seasoned compost, peat moss, or new potting soil.

December is the month to enjoy the beautiful poinsettias, Christmas cacti, holly and pyracantha berries, and early camellia blossoms.

Happy holidays! See you next year.

The Heart of the Matter

I read a newspaper article about a sizable survey concerning how the outdoors way of life compared with indoors urban living. According to this study, those having the advantage of sunlight, fresh air, and exercise are much healthier, happier, and better able to cope with stress compared to those who are compelled to work in offices or other restricted places. What a shame to have spent all that money on a survey when I could have given them that answer free of charge!

Even people who must spend most of their time indoors can improve their lives through gardening. Gardening encompasses a large choice of sites, activities, and plants in spaces ranging from pots and window boxes to many acres.

Plants are like people. Some we like better than others. So choose plants you react to positively.

But don't start with too many. They need tender, loving care each day. Learn all about the needs of those you choose, such as how much sun or shade each needs, how often to water and fertilize, what type of fertilizer is best, the ultimate size of a mature plant, seasonal color of foliage, correct pruning requirements, and what diseases and pests are most likely to invade. You'll also want to know whether your plants bloom and, if so, what color.

Gardening provides fresh air and exercise for people of all ages, sizes, and shapes. But one of the most important aspects of gardening to me is that it brings a sense of comradeship into our lives. Even though I never see most of my readers, I know that other people are experiencing much the same things that I am, which gives me a sense of fellowship with all of you. Gardening offers families, friends, and neighbors the opportunity to grow together.

Whatever kind of gardening you engage in, I hope this book will heighten your sense of wonder, peace, and joy.

Bibliography

Black, Dr. Robert J. [extension's urban horticulturist]. Monthly newsletter. University of Florida, Food and Agriculture Sciences, 1978–86.

Menninger, Edwin A. *Seaside Plants of the World.* New York: Hearthside Press, 1964.

Rare Fruit Council International, Tampa Bay Chapter. Monthly horticulture meetings and reports, 1981–90.

Rodale, J. I., ed. *Rodale's All-New Encyclopedia of Organic Gardening.* Emmaus, Penn.: Rodale, 1992.

Watkins, John V., and Thomas J. Sheehan. *Florida Landscape Plants.* Gainesville: University Press of Florida, 1975.

Watkins, John V., and Herbert S. Wolfe. *Your Florida Garden.* Gainesville: University Press of Florida, 1978.

Other Sources

Landscape Design School, Florida Federation of Garden Clubs. Two-year course for landscape design critics, 1977–79.

Thaddeus "Ted" Cyzycki [Florida gardening authority]. Gray's Garden Center, Ormond Beach, Fla., 1946–96.

University of Florida School of Horticulture, Gainesville. Short courses.

Index

❀

Page numbers in italics refer
to figures and tables.